verbatim

Jeremy Sims, Gillian Jones and and Jeff Truman in the 1993 Company B production of *Aftershocks*. (Photo: Paul Wright)

verbatim
Staging Memory & Community

edited by
PAUL BROWN

written by
CAROLINE WAKE
ROSLYN OADES
MEG MUMFORD
ULRIKE GARDE
PAUL DWYER
PAUL BROWN
JAMES ARVANITAKIS

interviews by
ROSLYN OADES

First published in 2010 by
Currency Press Pty Ltd
PO Box 2287
Strawberry Hills NSW 2012 Australia
www.currency.com.au
enquiries@currency.com.au

Copyright © Paul Brown, 2010

COPYING FOR EDUCATIONAL PURPOSES
The Australian *Copyright Act 1968* (Act) allows a maximum of one chapter or 10% of this book, whichever is the greater, to be copied by any educational institution for its educational purposes provided that that educational institution (or the body that administers it) has given a remuneration notice to Copyright Agency Limited (CAL) under the Act.
For details of the CAL licence for educational institutions contact CAL, Level 15, Castlereagh Street, Sydney, NSW, 2000. Tel: 1800 066 844; email: info@copyright.com.au

COPYING FOR OTHER PURPOSES
Except as permitted under the Act, for example a fair dealing for the purposes of study, research, criticism or review, no part of this book may be reproduced, stored in a retrieval system, or transmitted in any form or by any means without prior written permission. All enquiries should be made to the publisher at the address above.

National Library of Australia Cataloguing-in-Publication Data:
Title: Verbatim : staging memory and community / editor, Paul Brown ; writers, Caroline Wake ... [et al.]
ISBN: 9780868198798 (pbk.)
Notes: Includes bibliographical references.
Target Audience: For secondary school age.
Subjects: Improvisation (Acting)--Study and teaching (Secondary)--New South Wales.
               Drama in education--New South Wales.
               Theater--Study and teaching (Secondary)--New South Wales.
Other Authors/Contributors:
               Brown, Paul, 1952 Jan 21-
               Wake, Caroline.
Dewey Number: 792.028

Cover and book design by Emma Vine, Currency Press
Front cover shows: (top) Mitchell Butel and Russell Dykstra in the 2001 Company B production of *The Laramie Project*; (bottom background) Roxanne McDonald, Jeanette Cronin, Leah Purcell and Lisa Flanagan in the 2007 Company B production of *Parramatta Girls*; (foreground) Lisa Flanagan. Back cover shows the set of the 2007 Company B production of *Parramatta Girls* (all photos Heidrun Löhr).
Printed by Ligare Book Printers, Riverwood.

The book has been printed on paper certified by the Programme for the Endorsement of Forest Certification (PEFC). PEFC is committed to sustainable forest management through third party forest certification of responsibly managed forests.

Contents

Preface..vii

Website Material and Links.............................ix

Acknowledgements.......................................x

Important Note..xi

About the Authors...................................xiii

Part One: Verbatim and Documentary Theatre Practices: An Overview

    1. Towards a Working Definition of Verbatim Theatre...... 2
                                         Caroline Wake

    2. Verbatim Theatre within a Spectrum of Practices........ 6
                                         Caroline Wake

    3. A Short History of Verbatim Theatre................... 9
                  Ulrike Garde, Meg Mumford and Caroline Wake

    4. The Future of Verbatim Theatre: Truthfulness in a New Era.. 18
                            Paul Brown and Caroline Wake

    Exercises for Part One............................... 22

Part Two: Plays in the Curriculum

    5. *The Laramie Project*: Performing the Play in the United States of America and Australia........................... 25
                                         Caroline Wake

    6. *Aftershocks:* Voices from a Shaken Community........ 37
                                       Meg Mumford

    7. *Minefields and Miniskirts*: Women's Voices and the Vietnam War... 49
                                           Paul Brown

    8. *Parramatta Girls*: Verbatim Theatre about the Forgotten Australians...................................... 59
                                         Roslyn Oades

    9. *Run Rabbit Run*: Voices from the Heartland of Rugby League... 67
                                           Paul Dwyer

Part Three: Workshops for Exploring Themes and Issues

    10. Making a Verbatim Play........................... 79
                                           Paul Brown

    11. Creating a Headphone-Verbatim Performance........ 84
                                           Roslyn Oades

    12. Memory, Truth and Authenticity 88
                                           Ulrike Garde

    13. Theatricality and Engagement: Performing Real People 97
                                           Meg Mumford

    14. Verbatim Theatre and Community................. 103
                                        James Arvanitakis

    15. Ethics, Ownership, Authorship 109
                                           Paul Brown

Appendix 1: Interview Technique 113

Appendix 2: Sample Interview Release Forms.............. 117

Endnotes 119

Bibliography 123

Preface

During the twentieth century humans acquired a new skill. Aided by all manner of portable recording devices, we learnt how to tell a 'people's history' by capturing the real voices (with or without images) of our families or strangers, of famous monarchs or ordinary citizens, of those confronting crises and trauma or people negotiating everyday life. The origins of verbatim theatre lie in this alignment of new technologies with ancient storytellers' craft, which brought new dimensions to oral traditions of sharing human experience.

Recording real people's stories and thereby using their words to make a script for actors to perform is the fundamental craft of verbatim theatre. This book is an exploration of this form of drama, which emerged in the second half of the twentieth century, and remains very much alive, evolving and contemporary today. With its associated web material, our book is intended for both teachers and students studying and making verbatim theatre at senior high school level. It is also valuable for theatre practitioners intrigued by verbatim and wanting to devise new works.

The contributing authors bring the perspective of educators and analysts, but equally their practical experience as theatre workers. We embarked on the project in the same way we might begin any collectively-devised creative work: with meetings in coffee shops and bookstores and rehearsal rooms. We have been informed by practical workshops we have run for teachers, students and theatre workers, and we have consulted high school drama teachers to ensure we were on track.

The key focus of this book is the selection of verbatim plays set for Higher School Certificate drama in New South Wales, though the book is also relevant for the curriculum in other Australian States, and potentially for the forthcoming national drama curriculum. While the book explores a wide range of 'Reality Plays', we give close attention to interpreting the rubric that is the Topic 8 curriculum, and the verbatim plays prescribed by that curriculum. This strongly implies workshop-led teaching built around the set texts and the practical experience of verbatim theatre.

Part One of this book explores definitions, history and context for verbatim theatre. In Part Two, we provide project and production history, commentary and analysis, reviews and audience reactions for the five set plays:

- *The Laramie Project*
- *Aftershocks*
- *Minefields and Miniskirts*
- *Parramatta Girls*
- *Run Rabbit Run*

Each play is explored in its social context, and in the context of documentary and 'real life' forms of contemporary drama. A feature of this book is the inclusion of extracts of interviews with creators of the plays, and these interviews can be heard or read in full on the www.currency.com.au/verbatimwebsite.aspx.

In Part Three, this book teases out the key challenges of verbatim theatre, through short essays, workshop material and class exercises, considering:

- Memory, truth and authenticity
- Theatricality and engagement in the creative process
- Social context and community involvement in verbatim and other reality plays
- Ethical issues associated with the making of verbatim plays

We have kept in mind that 'Verbatim' as a topic will usually be taught within one term of ten weeks, and we have tried to match the scope and depth of our book to take this into account. We know how important the set plays are for HSC students. However, the most sophisticated response to the topic of 'Verbatim' will be from students who can approach the set plays through their own experience of verbatim workshops, and who can show they know about the world from which these types of plays arise. This informs our exploration of both practice and context with regard to the set plays and related traditions.

Paul Brown
August 2010

Website Material and Links

This book has an associated website, hosted by Currency Press: www.currency.com.au/verbatimwebsite.aspx

The website is evolving. It includes interview transcripts with creative artists associated with each curriculum play, and you can access the original sound tapes of these interviews. It also contains critical analysis of each play, e.g. press reviews, academic articles, additional photographs and other images. There are links to other relevant websites, and in stages across coming years, we will add extra workshop material, seminar presentations by verbatim creators, and contributions from schools working on verbatim.

Teachers will also want to read this book in conjunction with New South Wales Department of Education and Training, HSC Drama Prescriptions 2010–2012, Topic 8 Verbatim Theatre Teachers' Notes, available at www.curriculumsupport.education.nsw.gov.au/secondary/creativearts/assets/drama/pdf/verbatim.pdf

Acknowledgements

We tested ideas and materials at workshops run by the National Institute of Dramatic Art, with thanks to Jacqui Cowell; likewise we thank the NSW Drama Teachers Association and Drama NSW for the chance to explore verbatim in their workshops during 2009 and 2010. Thanks in particular to the participants in these workshops and other drama teachers who gave advice.

Our sincere gratitude to Deborah Franco, Claire Grady, Emma Vine, Sian Jenkins and Kavita Bedford at Currency Press; also to Erica Pezzutti for interview transcripts.

Important Note

The website for HSC Drama Prescriptions (www.curriculumsupport. education.nsw.gov.au/secondary/creativearts/assets/drama/pdf/verbatim. pdf) includes 'Advice to teachers about working with controversial plays in the Year 12 Drama classroom', and we refer readers of this book to that guidance. Perhaps more than other Drama topics in the school curriculum, studying verbatim theatre opens up possibilities for making new plays on local issues based on real people's lives within school communities and neighbourhoods; and this book indicates methods for embarking on such projects. Verbatim techniques allow exploration of crises or matters of injustice or real life controversy; and this type of work can sometimes involve sensitive, disturbing and personal material. This means care is needed on the part of all participants in workshops, interviews and other aspects of making verbatim plays. Examples include the need for release forms which clarify the project for interviewees, establish who owns stories and scripts, and secures permission to use material. Sometimes there is a need to debrief interviewers who may encounter troubling material. We have included discussion of such issues within this book, but there is no substitute for careful consideration on a project by project basis.

Julie Hamilton and Josef Ber in the 2004 Company B production of *Run Rabbit Run*. (Photo: Heidrun Löhr)

About the Authors

PAUL BROWN is the co-author of *Aftershocks*, verbatim theatre about the Newcastle earthquake. Also an academic, he is based in the School of History and Philosophy at the University of New South Wales (UNSW). He co-founded Urban Theatre Projects (formerly Death Defying Theatre) in 1980, and wrote major community theatre works for the Murray River Performing Group, Theatreworks, and Urban Theatre Projects. Paul is the author of the verbatim play *Half a Life*, which documents the experience of veterans who served at the British Nuclear Testing ground at Maralinga.

CAROLINE WAKE completed her PhD in theatre and performance studies at UNSW. Her research examines Australian documentary and verbatim theatre made by, with, and about asylum seekers. She is the co-editor of a special double issue of Performance Paradigm titled *After Effects: Performing the Ends of Memory* (2009). Her work has also appeared in *Research in Drama Education*. Outside academe, she is regular contributor to RealTime arts magazine and has trained and performed with PACT Theatre.

ROSLYN OADES is an experienced theatre director, performer, voice artist and community artist. She has created and directed two headphone-verbatim works with Urban Theatre Projects & BYDS: *Fast Cars & Tractor Engines* (2005) and *Stories of Love & Hate* (2008). She is currently working on her third in a trilogy on courageous acts titled, *I'm Your Man*.

MEG MUMFORD is a lecturer in Theatre and Performance Studies at UNSW. She has published extensively on the theory and practice of Bertolt Brecht, and is the author of the volume on Brecht in the Routledge Performance Practitioners Series (2009). Her main areas of expertise are German theatre and dance theatre since the nineteenth century, and the politics of performing bodies, translation, and intercultural exchange. She is currently working with Ulrike Garde on a comparative analysis of recent reality theatre from contemporary Australia and Germany, including forms such as documentary and verbatim theatre.

PAUL DWYER is the Chair of the Department of Performance Studies at Sydney University. An international authority on the work of Augusto Boal, he has published in *New Theatre Quarterly*, *Modern Drama*, *Research in Drama Education*, *Australasian Drama Studies* and other leading journals. Paul is also the dramaturg for the contemporary performance ensemble Version 1.0 (www.versiononepointzero.com) with whom he has created a number of critically acclaimed verbatim/documentary productions, including *CMI (A Certain Maritime Incident)*, *The Wages of Spin*, *Deeply Offensive and Utterly Untrue* and *The Bougainville Photoplay Project*.

ULRIKE GARDE is a theatre analyst. She is the Senior Lecturer in German Studies, in the European Languages and Cultures at Macquarie University, Sydney. Her research background is in German Studies and Cultural Studies, in particular the question of creating cultural identities in literature, the performing arts and critical reviews. In recent years, she has researched Australian-German cross-cultural relationships with a focus on the Australian reception of drama by German-speaking playwrights.

JAMES ARVANITAKIS is a social commentator and academic, whose work spans environmental issues, social justice advocacy and community work. He researches globalisation, citizenship, young people, security and the cultural commons, incorporating issues around hope, trust and safety. He has held positions with human rights-based organisations including AID/WATCH and Oxfam. James has also worked with playwrights and artists to document stories of injustice, including the Maralinga project *Half a Life*, which records the stories of nuclear veterans.

Part One

Verbatim and Documentary Theatre Practices: an Overview

Tracy Bartram, Debra Byrne, Tracy Mann, Wendy Stapleton and Robyn Arthur in the 2004 Playbox Theatre production of *Minefields and Miniskirts*. (Photo: Lisa Tomasetti)

1.
Towards a Working Definition of Verbatim Theatre

Caroline Wake

When we were drafting this book, playwright and director Roslyn Oades interviewed other playwrights and directors, as well as actors and designers, about how they defined the term 'verbatim theatre'. Here are some of their responses:

> **KATE GAUL: [DIRECTOR]** I guess broadly you would say stories drawn from real life and then I think you can become more specific about what that means from thenceforward. Um, there is a sense that the word 'verbatim' has something to do with words, that it's as reported, but of course a verbatim play is never word for word what was said, I wouldn't have thought. Ah, verbatim – I'd say stories from real life, from reality. Not made up.
>
> **ELIZA LOGAN: [ACTOR]** It's usually a play that, well I've only done a couple but of the ones that I've done the commonalities are true people's stories, usually revolving around a theme that means specifically something to the community. So something that's at the heart of the community, then whoever has created the production has then, um, created a piece of theatre out of that by interviewing people that are touched the most.
>
> **ALANA VALENTINE: [PLAYWRIGHT]** For me it's usually work that draws in some way from real life or a community – that's the first thing. The second thing is that it has a commitment to put that, the voice of that community um, on stage with, with some felicity to the way they speak... That's the second thing and the third thing is, I suppose, it's work which I consider has some ethical obligation back to that community to try and keep them involved in what you see on stage. So they're the three things that I think are really important about verbatim. So for me it's not just technically, literally, verbatim, that is representing their actual words, but it's kind of got those other components.

PAUL BROWN: [PLAYWRIGHT] Making taped interviews, transcribing them very very carefully, with every um and ah and pause, everything, left in the transcript and... applying the rule that the only words that the actors would speak had to be constructed out of those interviews.

Not only do these transcriptions help us to define verbatim theatre, they also hint at how verbatim theatre works. When we read these transcriptions aloud we can hear particular speaking patterns and rhythms. Even more intriguingly, we can follow an individual's train of thought, taking in their hesitations, reiterations and asides. Though we can't necessarily hear their accent or ascertain their cultural background, we can nevertheless begin to hear what Brown calls their 'voiceprints'.

Voiceprints are like fingerprints, in the sense that they are utterly unique and almost impossible to reproduce. Yet this is exactly what verbatim theatre attempts to do: to capture and reproduce voices; to give voice to people who might otherwise go voiceless or 'to give listening ears to voices that often go unheard' to paraphrase Robin Soans; and to tell stories that might otherwise go untold.[1] But who is the author of this story? Is it Roslyn Oades, the person who conducted the interview? Or is it Gaul, Logan, Valentine and Brown: the people speaking? Or maybe it's me, Caroline Wake, since I edited and arranged the recorded material. Or are we all authors – interviewers, interviewees, and editors? Some might even argue that the reader or spectator who makes sense of the verbatim material is another type of author.

In our own way, we have just written a very small verbatim play and hinted at some of the many issues involved: issues of voice, voiceprint, authorship, and authenticity. Of course, most verbatim plays are far more interesting than this one! However, the basic principle remains the same: the playwright or team of researchers records an interview with someone; they transcribe this interview; they place it alongside other interviews; they copy and paste, cut and edit these interviews into the script that has dramatic shape. Once they have a draft script they might conduct a rehearsed reading of it, so that the interviewees have a chance to see how they are going to be represented on stage and to give feedback to the playwright. Eventually, after consultation and negotiation, the script stabilises, at which point the actors and directors can start to prepare for more public performances. Beyond this brief description, what exactly is verbatim theatre, who invented it, and why should we study it?

In 1987, Derek Paget, writing in the journal *New Theatre Quarterly*, reviewed verbatim theatre as it evolved in Britain across the second half of the twentieth century. No-one, including Paget, wants to tightly restrict the meaning of 'verbatim theatre'. However, Paget does characterise it as theatre in which the company commits to the use of recorded, vernacular speech and to scrupulous use of historical evidence; and this is how verbatim playwrights generally proceed. Paget states that verbatim theatre is

> a form of theatre firmly predicated upon the taping and subsequent transcription of interviews with 'ordinary' people, done in the context of research into a particular region, subject area, issue, event, or combination of these things. This primary source is then transformed into a text which is acted, usually by the performers who collected the material in the first place.[2]

Paget was writing more than twenty years ago and a lot of things have changed since then. For instance, not every verbatim playwright transcribes their interviews; Roslyn Oades creates her plays by cutting and pasting audio samples rather than using snippets of copied out interviews (see Chapter 11: Creating a Headphone-Verbatim Performance). Similarly, not all plays are performed by the people who collected the interview material. Sometimes this happens because the playwright/s prefers to conduct all of the interviews themselves before creating a script to hand over to the actors. Other times this happens because the play is being restaged, outside its original context. So, for example, in the Sydney performance of *The Laramie Project*, none of the actors had been involved in conducting the interviews.

Nevertheless, one thing has remained the same over the past two decades and that is the importance of what Paget calls 'feeding back'. He says that more often than not verbatim plays are 'fed back into the communities (which have, in a real sense, created them), via performance in those communities'.[3] There are two ways in which verbatim plays can be fed back into their communities: (1) during the process of making the play; and (2) in the process of performing it. When making a verbatim play, the playwright and actors often organise a staged reading of the play in draft form. This gives the interviewees and other members of the community a chance to see how the play is shaping up. It also gives them the opportunity to voice any concerns and to tell the actors, directors and writers what they do and don't like: in this way the community can change the play. The second way in which a play is fed back into the community is through the more public performances at the end of the process. Here, the wider community can listen to a story about an issue or an event that has affected them, and pause to reflect on what has happened since then: in this way the play might change the community. Once again, practices differ and some playwrights might not have the time to do a staged reading, though this is not a recommended practice. Other playwrights might not be able to perform the play in the community that produced it. For instance, David Hare created his one-man play, *Via Dolorosa*, in conversation with Palestinians and Israelis, yet the play premiered in London in 1998 and played in New York in 1999 before it ever made it to Tel Aviv or Gaza. In this way, *Via Dolorosa* not only *represented* communities, it also *created* (temporary) communities by drawing people together for an evening to sit and think about a far away place.

Though their processes may differ, verbatim playwrights agree that the process of *making* a verbatim play is as important as *performing* it. In this sense, the 'term *verbatim* refers to the origins of the text spoken in the play' rather than to the final product. Indeed, the final products can vary widely. For this reason, Hammond and Steward argue that 'verbatim is not a form, it is a technique; it is a means rather than an end' and they point out that the end products can vary widely.[4] This emphasis on process also affects the audience and how they watch verbatim plays. For example, when we watch more conventional plays which have been written by a single author, we don't tend to think about who the playwright might have consulted and whether this was done in an ethical and responsible manner. When we see a verbatim play, however, we often wonder about how the playwright met these people, how they interacted with the community, and to what extent they collaborated with the community. In other words, we wonder about issues of authority, authenticity, truth, reality and ethics in a way that we don't always do when watching a play by, say, Chekhov.

It is clear from these preliminary definitions that there is a wide range of verbatim theatre practices. Maybe we should talk about verbatim theatres in the plural rather than verbatim theatre in the singular. Just as there are many ways of making verbatim theatre, there are also many ways of talking about verbatim theatre. In the following chapters we offer two ways in which you can begin thinking about verbatim theatre. In Chapter Two, we place verbatim theatre alongside related 'reality theatre' practices such as autobiographical performance, community theatre, documentary theatre, tribunal plays, and historical plays. That is, we offer a spectrum of theatre practices in which verbatim theatre can be located. Then in Chapter Three, we talk about verbatim theatre in terms of its history and trace the development of documentary and verbatim theatre over the course of the twentieth and twenty-first centuries.

2.

Verbatim Theatre within a Spectrum of Practices
Caroline Wake

Verbatim theatre is only one of many types of theatre that respond to and represent real people and events. While some people use documentary theatre as an umbrella term to cover all of these practices, others prefer terms such as the 'theatre of fact',[5] 'theatre of testimony',[6] or 'theatre of actuality'.[7] In the United States, scholars tend to use the term 'documentary theatre' to refer to all non-fiction theatre and they rarely use the term 'verbatim'. However, in the United Kingdom there is a tendency to distinguish between verbatim and documentary theatre. For our part, we are going to use Meg Mumford and Ulrike Garde's term 'reality theatre' as an overarching term and the terms 'verbatim' and 'documentary' to refer to particular theatre practices within that broader category.

Within the category of reality theatre there are a number of sub-categories, including autobiographical performance, community, and tribunal theatre. We have placed these along a continuum of reality theatre practices below.

Reality Theatre					
Autobiographical	Community	Verbatim	Documentary	Tribunal	History

We have devised this spectrum on the basis of the distance between the actual person and the writer. So, for instance, sitting at one end of the spectrum we have autobiographical plays where the real person and the writer are one and the same. Though they may deal with community issues, they do not necessarily consult with or interview the community.

Further along the spectrum, we have community theatre practices where performances are made by, with, and about community members. In addition, these plays often cast community members as themselves. For instance, in the United Kingdom, a group called Quarantine devised a performance titled *The Soldier's Song*, which featured currently serving soldiers as performers. An Australian example is Urban Theatre Project's play *Asylum*, which told the story of several refugees who had been held in immigration detention centres. Like autobiographical performers, these people played themselves and told their own stories.

In the middle we have verbatim theatre, which typically involves a playwright and actors interviewing the community about an issue or event that has affected them. Sometimes these people might play themselves, as happened in the Australian play *Through the Wire* in which Shahin Shafaei played himself. Other times, however, the actors who conducted their interviews might play the interviewees. Still other times, actors who have never met the interviewees might play them. The situation can vary from play to play.

Sitting on the other side of verbatim theatre is documentary theatre. Like verbatim plays, documentary plays both respond to and represent reality but they are arguably more hybrid because they include a variety of documents rather than just interviews. (In fact, it would be possible to construct a documentary play without doing interviews, as we will see in the next category.) Peter Weiss, German theatre practitioner, argues that this variety is vital to documentary theatre. Writing in 1968, he defined documentary theatre as:

> [A] theatre of reportage. Records, documents, letters, statistics, market-reports, statements by banks and companies, government statements, speeches, interviews, statements by well-known personalities, newspaper and broadcast reports, photos, documentary films and other contemporary documents are the basis of the performance. Documentary Theatre refrains from all invention; it takes authentic material and puts it on the stage, unaltered in content, edited in form. On the stage we show a selection based on a definite theme, generally of a social or political character, which contrasts with the haphazard nature of the news with which we are bombarded daily on all sides. This critical selection, and the principles by which the montage of snippets of reality is effected, determines the quality of documentary drama.[8]

This is probably the most commonly cited definition of documentary theatre, but it is not the only one. For example, the American theatre scholar Attilio Favorini defines documentary drama as:

> Plays characterized by a central or exclusive reliance on actual rather than imaginary event, on dialogue, song and/or visual materials (photographs, films, pictorial documents) 'found' in the historical record or gathered by the playwright/researcher, and by a disposition to set individual behavior in an articulate political and/or social context.[9]

The English theatre practitioner Peter Cheeseman is less strident in his tone and talks about objectivity. Favorini summarises it nicely when he says 'In contrast with the German documentarians of the 1960s [such as Weiss], Cheeseman is concerned with creating an audience of listeners rather than an audience of believers'.[10]

While documentary plays are based on a variety of sources, tribunal plays are based solely on the 'official transcripts of judicial proceedings'.[11] These proceedings may be a court case, a parliamentary inquiry or royal commission. Reinelt argues that tribunal plays are 'the theatrical equivalents of the 1960s "direct cinema": attempting objective reportage, removing all marks of the film-maker of the film, claiming the "high ground of science to support its superiority"'.[12] That is, they attempt to achieve some sort of objectivity, rather than presenting the material in the more subjective manner of Weiss.

Perhaps the most significant difference between verbatim and tribunal plays is that tribunal playwrights rarely conduct interviews. This is worth thinking about in more detail: verbatim playwrights pride themselves on telling stories that aren't being told elsewhere and they often describe what they are doing with phrases such as 'hidden histories', 'giving voice to the voiceless', or 'writing from the ground up'. In contrast, tribunal playwrights are retelling stories that have already been told. Instead of telling a hidden history, they re-examine official history; re-staging an inquiry so that we the audience can re-view and, indeed, review it. In Carol Martin's words, tribunal plays 'reopen trials in order to critique justice'.[13]

Here, we reach the other end of our spectrum of reality theatres. The last category, the history play, is probably a bit of a stretch as the writers of history plays consult historical documents but tend not to incorporate them into their play. Nevertheless, history plays are still worth thinking about since they often deal with actual events. Favorini, for instance, argues that the plays of Herodotus, Phrynichus, and Aeschylus all deal with contemporary events in Ancient Greece and all demonstrate what he calls the 'documentary impulse', even though they aren't, strictly speaking, documentaries. He also argues that the documentary impulse can be seen in the plays of the Elizabethan era, when Shakespeare wrote chronicles of the English royalty and other writers created tragic dramas inspired by contemporary 'true crime'. More recently, Paget has coined the term 'docudrama' and the acronym 'BOATS', which stands for Based On A True Story, to refer to plays that take their cue from reality but do not adhere to it too strictly. In other words, though they are loosely based on real events, history plays take significant liberties with the facts and do not necessarily consult with the community.

Looking at all of these categories, it is arguable that *The Laramie Project* is not, strictly speaking, a verbatim play! Rather, it is a hybrid: mostly verbatim but also part documentary (it incorporates bits of media footage and photographs), and part tribunal (it incorporates bits of courtroom transcripts). However, other plays on the list, such as *Aftershocks*, are arguably very 'pure' verbatim plays. Indeed, *Aftershocks* is constructed solely from interviews and only combines the speech of interviewees very occasionally. Other plays, like Alana Valentine's *Parramatta Girls*, sit somewhere between the two: drawing on interviews like Paul Brown does in *Aftershocks*, but taking the occasional liberty by creating characters that are composites of several interviewees.

3.
A Short History of Verbatim Theatre
ULRIKE GARDE, MEG MUMFORD AND CAROLINE WAKE

In the previous chapter we developed a system of classification for the spectrum of 'reality' theatres. In doing so, we hinted at the history of verbatim theatre by mentioning names such as Peter Weiss, Peter Cheeseman, and Derek Paget. In this section we go into more detail, looking at not only *who* developed verbatim theatre, but also *how* it developed, *where*, *when*, and *why*. To put it another way, while the last section looked at verbatim theatre's siblings, this section looks at its parents and grandparents and the worlds they lived in.

You will soon realise that this chapter has most to say about 'documentary theatre', since this is the title most commonly used in literature about the relatives of verbatim theatre. Also, we must warn you this is a necessarily abbreviated history of documentary and verbatim theatre. For a more comprehensive account, we suggest looking first at the 1995 book edited by Attilio Favorini titled *Voicings: Ten Plays from the Documentary Theater*.

Finding voices from everyday life: Storm and Stress

While the Western interest in staging contemporary reality is as old as Ancient Greek theatre, verbatim theatre's emphasis on the careful attention to voices from everyday life began to emerge in the more recent Sturm and Drang, or Storm and Stress, drama of late eighteenth-century Germany. It was the rebellion of the young Storm and Stress playwrights – such as the early Schiller (1759–1805), Goethe (1749–1832) and Lenz (1751–92) – against the forms and ideas of Neoclassical art that marked the emergence of a mainstream realist theatre attentive to the literal words of the people. In contrast to the Neoclassical insistence on presenting universal truths and eternal norms – through poetic verse, elitist forms of official High German language, coherent stock types, and unified five-act dramas – these forerunners of Weimar Classicism and the Romantics attempted to address the reality of human changeability, diversity and uniqueness.

Inspired by Shakespeare and influenced by new understandings about the way each individual was shaped by particular social, historical, biological and psychological forces, the Storm and Stress playwrights experimented with innovative ways of representing human idiosyncrasy. Much to the dismay of the arbiters of taste, they began to use idiomatic prose peppered with colloquialisms, slang, incomplete sentences and even obscenities.

No longer were their tragedies populated exclusively by members of the aristocracy, but the mythological kings and queens began to be upstaged by contemporary soldiers, artists and private tutors who walked and talked very much like the contemporary people their authors had read about in newspapers or observed first-hand.

The first docudramas

It was Georg Büchner (1813–37) who arguably began to craft the first plays to resemble documentary drama. A medical scientist and left-wing activist, Büchner also pursued his interest in social order, health and justice through writing drama and literature closely based on documents from recent history. Over one sixth of *Danton's Death* (1835), a type of history play that deals with a dark period of social disorder during the French Revolution, consists of paraphrased or verbatim quotations from historical texts containing primary source materials.[14] In 1835 he also finished *Lenz*, a prose narrative based on a pastor's diary entries, which has been hailed as the first classical study of schizophrenia. Just before Büchner's untimely death in 1837 from typhus, he was working on *Woyzeck*, a working-class tragedy focused on a low-ranking soldier who, afflicted by poverty, malnutrition, and jealousy, murders the mother of his child. The incomplete play draws on documentation surrounding three early nineteenth-century murder cases, especially medical reports about the mental state and accountability of the historical Johann Christian Woyzeck. All of these texts were guided by Büchner's belief that the dramatist's 'supreme task is to get as close as possible to history as it actually happened'.[15]

Büchner's use of documents and first-hand observation to create realistic behaviour, and to give voice to contemporary issues and people marginalised on the main stage, was developed further by the late nineteenth-century European Naturalists. Playwrights such as Émile Zola (1840–1902), Gerhart Hauptmann (1862–1946), Henrik Ibsen (1828–1906), August Strindberg (1849–1912) and Anton Chekhov (1860–1904), all sought to address sides of contemporary life not openly or adequately addressed in public life – from alcoholism and syphilis to urban social deprivation and the battle of the sexes – through a form of writing that created idiosyncratic voiceprints. Theatre-makers including André Antoine (1858–1943), Constantin Stanislavsky (1863–1948), and Otto Brahm (1856–1912) staged many of the Naturalists' plays with the assistance of new technologies that enabled them to have access to documents such as prints, photos, transcriptions of phonograph recordings, and to the far-flung people and milieu being represented. However, rather than carrying out interviews exactly mimicking the form and content of an interviewee's speech and seeking out participant feedback, all of these practitioners tended to assert their own authorial vision through the independent scripting and staging of imagined or 'factitional' characters, dialogue and events.

Political theatre and new technologies

In the 1920s the political theatre of Erwin Piscator (1893–1966), often regarded as the founding father of modern documentary theatre, and *recordings* of people and events played a far more prominent role in plays that exploited the capacities of the slide projector and film to address topical social issues. These new technologies featured in Piscator's 1925 co-production, together with Felix Gasbarra, of *In Spite of Everything!*, a political revue commissioned by the German Communist Party. This staging of the ten-year history of the party helped forge a new form of theatre, one composed entirely of visual and verbal documents.[16] In Favorini's word, Piscator's innovation was to:

> create a drama based on the principles of news reportage, constructed in an epic succession of tableaux and stations, and designed to promote direct social action. Presented in a revue format and accompanied by music, political cartoons, moving pictures borrowed from government archives and photographic projections, *In Spite of Everything!* created an alternative to the capitalist newspaper accounts of the same events.[17]

Thus, from its very beginnings, documentary theatre is deeply entangled with politics, technology and an oppositional or questioning attitude towards mainstream media. The same can be said of verbatim theatre, emerging, as we'll see, from opposing politics following World War II.

Troubled times and Living Newspapers

The interwar period (1918–1939) was marked by the birth and interbreeding of many new members of the 'reality' family, a symptom of the thirst for useful and responsible art in a turbulent period of social change. Most of Piscator's productions prior to the Great Depression of the late 1920s were spectacular versions of their Eastern European cousins, the Living Newspaper shows of the USSR's Blue Blouse theatre troupes. These sketches, which Derek Paget describes as the first documentary dramas, were commissioned by the Department of Agitation and Propaganda (Agitprop) to present facts and information about the progress of the Russian revolution to a vast and, for the most part, illiterate population.[18] Though they started as simple oral readings of the newspaper, the Living Newspapers became increasingly animated and soon started to incorporate slides, songs and segments of film. Piscator was aware of this Agitprop work, and a Blue Blouse troupe toured to his Berlin theatre in 1927.

The process of cross-fertilisation extended to North America through the Federal Theatre Project (FTP). This was a United States-government-funded initiative under President Roosevelt that sought to support theatre and other performing arts projects during the Depression, thereby keeping artists employed and struggling families entertained. Though the quality of the work varied, the FTP's most famous form was its version of the Living

Newspaper – socially-engaged plays adapted from newspaper reports by unemployed journalists and theatre-makers. Links between key figures in the FTP and the left-wing club Unity Theatre (1936–83), initially based in London, contributed to the development of British Living Newspapers and other documentary pieces which drew attention to the victims of the Depression as well as challenging the totalitarian political regimes that dominated the landscapes of World War II.

The second wave of documentary theatre

Rather than being effectively opposed, totalitarian politics got the upper hand and as a result the developing tradition of political documentary theatre was halted in many corners of the world. European practitioners such as Piscator were forced into exile, and North American supporters of political theatre were silenced by anti-communist investigations such as the House Un-American Activities Committee which contributed to the demise of the FTP in 1939. But the traditions of documentary theatre re-emerged in the 1960s, another period of social unrest and heightened political awareness marked by phenomena such as the 1968 student revolutions, the Civil Rights and Anti-Vietnam War movements, and Cold War terrorist attacks on capitalism and the legacy of fascism. As West Germany was at the heart of these battles, it is perhaps not surprising that it dominated the second wave of documentary theatre.

Both the first and the second wave of documentary theatre in Germany have been attributed to socio-political circumstances. According to Brian Barton, the periods between 1924–29 and 1963–70 were times in which burning social and political questions

> were considered too urgent, too complex or too overwhelming for fictional plots or characters being able to deal with them adequately. Under these circumstances, artistic truth needs to be certified by concrete documentary evidence.[19]

New forms

In West Germany, after World War II, a new generation critically assessed its parent's involvement in the atrocities of the Nazi regime, and the student movement protested against established value systems. In this context, documentary approaches represented a turning point from apolitical towards politically-engaged theatre. Several playwrights considered 'pure' fiction as inadequate for capturing past traumatic events or burning contemporary political questions. Instead, the various documentary forms turned theatre into an instrument for sharing and critically re-assessing knowledge and information.

This critical function of theatre is obvious in Rolf Hochhuth's 1962 play *The Representative* (or *The Deputy*): not only was it the first German documentary drama to be performed in Australia, it also received three separate productions in 1965.[20] All over the world, the related performances caused heated debates over the play's central question, which was whether the late Pope Pius XII had a duty to speak out publicly against the extermination of European Jews during the Nazi time.

Both *The Representative* and Peter Weiss' *The Investigation* were written nearly twenty years after the end of World War II. The latter play needs to be interpreted in the historical context of the Frankfurt Auschwitz trials (1963–5), the largest trial of Holocaust perpetrators conducted in West German courts. Weiss wanted the Holocaust to be part of our collective memory (see Chapter 12: Memory, Truth and Authenticity) and he tried to invite critical engagement by using aesthetics which were reminiscent of Brecht's 'defamiliarisation effects'. These aim to create a critically distanced attitude to the subject matter of the performance. Weiss organised *The Investigation* as an 'Oratorio in Eleven Cantos' in which the characters represent different members of society and different stakeholder groups. One way in which this play diverges from 'pure' verbatim theatre is that its language does not imitate individual voiceprints. Instead, the neutral language is arranged in verse form.

Another play with a mixed approach to documentary techniques is Heinar Kipphardt's *In the Matter of J. Robert Oppenheimer* (1964). It balances the tension between 'truthfulness' and creative audience engagement by using a combination of documentary elements such as slides, tapes and film clips with dramatically-crafted monologues. The playwright's subject matter focused on the McCarthy era and the transcripts of the 1954 hearings of the Security Board of Atomic Energy. The plot is based on Oppenheimer's refusal to participate in the creation of a hydrogen bomb in 1951.

During the same period in Britain, Joan Littlewood and her Theatre Workshop collaborators were reinvigorating aspects of the epic documentary tradition. Littlewood and Ewan MacColl had been producing forms such as Living Newspaper since they founded Theatre for Action in Manchester in 1934, a company dedicated to the task of bringing theatre to the working classes. Reinvented as Theatre Workshop in 1945, and based from 1952 at the Theatre Royal Stratford East in London, the company aimed to engender communal solidarity and to provide the under-represented with a voice in society. The documentary piece for which they won acclaim was the 1963 production *Oh! What a Lovely War*, a group-devised critique of capitalist (business) warfare that was structured around the presentation of a diverse array of World War I songs. A hybrid piece, the work combined music hall entertainment with memoirs, factual data, and projected images of maps and soldiers in the trenches. Comments and war memorabilia offered by audience members were often incorporated into the script as the production developed. Not only did the show highlight the marginalised voices and language of the soldiers, but it also invited its local communities and visiting spectators to participate in its co-creation. Theatre Workshop was one of the models for British political theatre troupes such as John McGrath's 7:84 Theatre Company. Their most famous production was *The Cheviot, The Stag and the Black Black Oil* in 1973–5. This critical commentary on two hundred years of economic change in the Scottish highlands, mixed musical numbers with historical information, and toured to many of the communities whose social histories the play addresses.

Verbatim theatre becomes a distinct form

Perhaps the most significant development of the 1960s and 70s is that verbatim theatre began to break away from documentary theatre and become a distinct form in its own right. More than anyone else, Peter Cheeseman deserves the credit for this. Working in a town called Stoke-on-Trent, Cheeseman produced several plays by interviewing the community about issues and events that affected them, including *The Jolly Potters* (1964), *The Staffordshire Rebels* (1965), *The Knotty* (1966), *Six Into One* (1968), *The Burning Mountain* (1970), and *Fight for Shelton Bar* (1974). Unlike documentary theatre, which depends on media clippings and news footage, Cheeseman sought to create his own news by telling the stories that weren't being told elsewhere, and in his plays he avoided the use of projected documentary images. Significantly, it was in an article about Cheeseman's work that Derek Paget defined verbatim theatre.

Despite the flurry of activity in the United Kingdom, the 1960s and 70s didn't do much for documentary theatre in the United States, where it remained relatively unpopular. Only two documentary plays of note were staged: Martin Duberman's *In White America* (1963), which, as the title suggests, contemplated issues of race and racism; and Donald Freed's *The Inquest* (1970), which was based on the trial of Julius and Ethel Rosenberg. However, in the late-1970s and early-1980s, writer and director Emily Mann started to reinvigorate the form. In 1980 she produced the play *Still Life*, which was based on interviews with a Vietnam veteran, his wife, and his mistress. In 1984, she wrote *The Execution of Justice,* about the assassination of San Francisco Mayor George Moscone and gay City Supervisor Harvey Milk. (Interestingly enough, one character in *The Laramie Project*, Zackie Salmon, actually mentions this event (page 91) and the events have been depicted in the 2008 film *Milk*, directed by Gus Van Sant and starring Sean Penn. The play was based on the trial transcripts and buttressed by additional interviews with what Mann described as the 'uncalled' witnesses.[21]

In the 1990s, documentary theatre started to make a comeback in the United States, largely due to the work of Anna Deavere Smith. One of her most famous plays is *Fires in the Mirror* (1992), which deals with the Crown Heights riots in Brooklyn, New York. The riots broke out after a rabbi's motorcade ran over and killed a black boy, precipitating the killing of a

Jewish student in retaliation. In order to create the play, Smith interviewed more than twenty bystanders, community members, and leaders about the incident. She then performed as all of them in her one-woman show, shifting from one character to another simply by removing a hat or putting on glasses and changing her accent. Similarly, for her show *Twilight: Los Angeles* (1994), Smith interviewed several people from a variety of backgrounds about the violent aftermath of the Rodney King trial and verdict. Once again, she performed all of the characters.

Verbatim theatre in Australia

Significantly, the 1990s was also when verbatim theatre arrived in Australia. Though there had been some documentary plays staged during the 1950s and 1960s, and there had been many community plays that utilised oral history (you can listen to Paul Brown's interview on the Currency Press website), the first fully-fledged verbatim play was not staged until 1991. In that year, the Newcastle Workers Club inspired *Aftershocks*, a play based on interviews with staff and members of the Club about their experiences and memories of the Newcastle earthquake. It was first devised by the Workers Cultural Action Committee, which co-presented the first production with the Hunter Valley Theatre Company. Two years later, in 1993, Company B in Sydney produced the play with a new cast.

Since then, there have been a number of similar plays made with communities who are undergoing or recovering from crisis. In 2004 Alana Valentine's *Run Rabbit Run*, a play about the exclusion of the South Sydney Rabbitohs from the National Rugby League and the community's battle to be readmitted, premiered at Company B. Two years later, in 2006, another play steered by Paul Brown, *Half a Life*, premiered at the Ettalong Beach War Memorial Club. The play deals with the nuclear tests conducted in Central Australia and the effects that they have had on veterans and their families. Stories of disaster and war have also been told in *Sandakan Threnody* (2004), which deals with the experiences of prisoners of war held in Sandakan, Borneo, during World War II; *Minefields and Miniskirts* (2005), which deals with women's experiences of the Vietnam War; and Campion Decent's play *Embers* (2006), which is based on interviews with survivors of the 2003 Victorian bushfires. Similarly, indigenous stories have also been recounted in verbatim plays such as Valentine's *Parramatta Girls* (2007), which tells the stories of women who had been held in the Parramatta Girls Home. Together with *Minefields and Miniskirts*, as well as plays such as *Conversations in a Brothel* (2004) and *Bring a Nice Dress* (2005), which were based on interviews with Perth sex workers, you might also argue that *Parramatta Girls* forms part of a distinctly feminist strand of Australian verbatim theatre.

There have also been a number of verbatim plays created by, with, and about refugees and asylum seekers. One of the earliest plays was Urban Theatre Projects' production *Asylum*, which was devised and performed by people who had been held in detention centres. In 2002 and 2003, the activist group Actors for Refugees interviewed refugees in order to create two plays: *Club Refuge* and *Something to Declare: True Stories of Refugees and Asylum Seekers in Australia*. Also in 2002, Sydney's Sidetrack Theatre staged *Citizen X*, a play based on the letters from asylum seekers in detention centres rather than interviews with them. In 2004, these efforts started to move to the mainstream when Ros Horin's play *Through the Wire* premiered at the Sydney Festival. This play told the story of four asylum seekers, one of whom – Shahin Shafaei – played himself. That same year, Company B presented *In Our Name*, which was a collaboration between Nigel Jamieson and the Al Abbadi family. Unlike *Through the Wire*, however, the Al Abbadis did not appear to play themselves. That same year, the company Version 1.0 performed their tribunal play based on the transcripts of a parliamentary inquiry, called *CMI: A Certain Maritime Incident*. Since then, Version 1.0 have continued to experiment with the documentary and tribunal forms, also producing *Wages of Spin* (2005) about the war on terror, *From a Distance* (2006) about the reaction to Sally Robbins' rowing performance at the Olympics, *Deeply Offensive and Utterly Untrue* (2007) about the 'wheat for weapons' scandal, and *This Kind of Ruckus* (2009) about domestic violence.

During this time, Australia also saw local productions of some overseas verbatim plays such as Tectonic Theatre Project's *The Laramie Project* (2001), David Hare's *The Permanent Way* (2005), and *Stuff Happens* (2005). This is a really interesting aspect of verbatim theatre in Australia – we often perform verbatim plays from elsewhere. Since then, there has been little sign of the trend slowing down. Indeed, if anything it has accelerated, especially after the events of September 11 2001, when writers of all kinds – not just playwrights – seemed to turn from fiction towards non-fiction.

Summary: political and technological influences

Looking back over this brief history, we can see that the popularity of the various forms of reality theatre waxes and wanes. But what causes these fluctuations? One possible explanation is political. Documentary theatre seems to make a resurgence during politically turbulent times. For instance, in the 1960s, Germany was struggling to come to terms with World War II, some sectors of the population of the United States was starting to doubt its role in Vietnam, and the civil rights and feminist movements were starting to gain serious momentum. Likewise, in the 2000s, people were deeply divided over the aftermath of September 11 and the wars in Afghanistan and Iraq.

Sitting alongside this political explanation is a technological one, since the fate of documentary and verbatim theatres is tied to the technologies of recording. The Naturalist theatre of the late nineteenth century and the documentary theatre of the early twentieth century would not have been possible without the invention of film and projection. The verbatim theatre of Peter Cheeseman in the 1960s would not have come about without the invention of relatively small and inexpensive tape recorders. Likewise, it is arguable that the recent invention of mediatised verbatim or recorded delivery is tied to the development of digital recording. We have only scratched the surface of this new technology, and we are nowhere near using it to its full potential. There are so many interesting issues to consider: what happens when we put all the raw materials for a verbatim play – the original interviews, the transcripts, etc – on a website and let the audience put together their own play? What completely new ways of recording speech will emerge? What would a verbatim play look like in the imagined Internet world that is Second Life?

4.

The Future of Verbatim Theatre: Truthfulness in a New Era

PAUL BROWN AND CAROLINE WAKE

We've just ended the previous chapter with a challenge to think through the connections between verbatim theatre and the Internet and therefore the potential for further evolution of techniques and dramatic forms. Perhaps we should explore current trends and future possibilities a little more.

So far we have offered two ways of thinking about verbatim theatre: firstly in terms of other related practices; and secondly in terms of historical developments. In a different version of Part One of this book, we might have written a series of mini-introductions; offering you little histories of what has happened, is happening and is likely to happen in Germany, the United States, the United Kingdom and Australia. Or we could have taken up one of Favorini's suggestions, and considered verbatim theatre alongside narrative ballads, oral epics, folk and passion plays.[22]

Obviously there are many other approaches and vocabularies available to analyse verbatim theatre and consider its future. Some scholars talk about it as a form of 'oral history performance'[23] while others think about it as a form of 'performance ethnography', meaning that they think of the playwright as a sort of anthropologist, who goes to, observes and participates in a community before presenting the research in a play rather than a book, as most anthropologists do.[24] All these influences have some bearing on verbatim's future.

What are the trends? Where is verbatim theatre headed?

In *Verbatim Verbatim*, edited by Hammond and Steward, six key figures in British verbatim theatre explore the purpose and potential of verbatim techniques. Their essays and interviews are rich with examples – they reference some thirty verbatim plays with a variety of forms. These include the more traditional plays in which culled and edited transcripts become monologue and dialogue, the 'Tribunal' plays by Tricycle Theatre which select from and re-stage real-life courtroom transcripts, and Alecky Blythe's 'Recorded Delivery' performances, in which actors receive a 'feed' of original interviews via headphones.

In the evolving British tradition, something controversial overwrites the history and seems most urgent. It is a very confident assertion by practitioners that verbatim theatre displaces mainstream media as the form of documentation most likely to deliver 'truth'. According to these practitioners, the central purpose of verbatim work has gone well beyond the staging of 'hidden voices'. Now playwrights and companies using the form are intent on overcoming the deficit in reliable documentation that arises out of *globalisation*, for example the failed attempts by globalised media to provide citizens with truthful accounts of the Gulf Wars and the so-called War on Terror. When Tricycle Theatre produces *Called to Account: the indictment of Anthony Charles Lynton Blair for the crime of aggression against Iraq: a hearing*, they are staging the otherwise unattainable trial of a Prime Minister who lied to a nation.[25]

In *Verbatim Verbatim*, editors Hammond and Steward also indicate some key questions which are guiding the development of verbatim theatre, such as 'What passes for veracity in verbatim theatre?' Or 'What are the ethical issues in bringing real peoples' stories onto a public stage?' Or 'To what extent does the verbatim dramatist remain an author?' Or 'What are the implications of the mainstreaming of verbatim, with its attendant celebrity-making?' Or, 'Is verbatim superior to journalism?' None of these questions has a single answer, and we will come to them as we explore particular plays in Part Two of this book.

Audiences craving truth

Perhaps the last-mentioned question above, comparing verbatim to journalism, is the most important. We can note the decline of honesty in public life at the very time audiences crave truth; this is happening through the reduced capacity for truth-making in institutions, including the media, security agencies and government inquiries.[26] Expecting not to be lied to in verbatim theatre, its audiences listen more intently than in 'created plays' or 'fully imagined plays' (these being two labels Hammond and Steward propose for non-verbatim plays). Max Stafford-Clark proposes verbatim theatre audiences listen as if receiving truth via an 'aside' directed to the audience in Shakespeare or Restoration theatre.[27]

For verbatim audiences, the delivery to their ears of words from real people may be an antidote to the ethical crisis in journalism, a crisis journalists themselves admit to. Indeed some journalists, including British playwright Richard Norton-Taylor who hails from the *Guardian* newspaper, are crossing into verbatim theatre.

Verbatim Verbatim contains many other insights into the ongoing purpose of verbatim theatre. For example, David Hare and Max Stafford-Clark show how the audience become the 'play-makers', able to place real stories in broader social and political context. In the presence of actors telling stories, audiences re-construct the strange and interesting real world for themselves. Meanwhile, for practitioners, there remain questions to be addressed project by project, such as whether the playwright becomes a character, or at least 'present' through reference by other characters, as David Hare allows in *The Permanent Way*. As the genre evolves, more verbatim playwrights experiment with a certain amount of 'fictional' material; and when asked whether they 'cheat' on the process of accurate transcription, the consensus is best expressed by Robin Soans:

> Do I ever cheat? Is there ever a tension between being truthful to the interviewees and creating something that I know is going to work theatrically? The answer is yes, but not a lot.[28]

It seems all verbatim writers and directors will continue the difficult task of making dialogue scenes out of mostly monologue interviews, all will go on seeking ways to stage present action from stories told to them in past tense, and all will continue to search for comedy in what is usually distressing and confronting material. If we take on what practitioners say in *Verbatim Verbatim*, some will regard verbatim plays as short-lived, dealing well with current controversy but less intent on survival as 'art'. Others will find new ways to explore their work as enduring acts of creative imagination, though they draw from reality.

After around four decades of practice, verbatim theatre practitioners seem secure in their craft, agreeing it is akin to the art of a sculptor hewing beauty from a stone, using skills overlapping a documentary film editor's, while drawing on writer's tools for structuring and dramatisation. The days of seeing verbatim as second rate compared with other techniques are gone. With confidence David Hare claims verbatim's ability to arrest the 'drift towards less and less important subject matter in British theatre', while he praises 'the sheer seriousness and intensity with which [verbatim is] able to bring the theatre's special scrutiny to bear'.[29]

In search of justice

Ultimately, as Nicholas Kent says in *Verbatim, Verbatim*, the verbatim arena is populated by 'people who care about injustice' and because verbatim plays draw audiences which include opinion-formers and decision-makers, they exert influence and call for justice well beyond the theatre.[30] In exposing injustice, Richard Norton-Taylor suggests verbatim (eg Tribunal) plays, through their two hour presentations, lie in a 'convenient space somewhere between the several months (or even longer) of tribunal testimony and the cursory reports offered in the daily media'.[31] In what we might see as the modern era of verbatim, in which truthfulness and the politics of injustice guide the work, the power to influence decision-makers is all important, drawing on knowledge made in the playmaking processes linking real life to staged performance. Richard Norton-Taylor summarises how this works:

> First [...] a group of actors on a stage [...] give a sense of context much more effectively than the written word alone. The experience of watching leads to an understanding that goes beyond the mere

intake of information; it involves empathy for the victims. Second... witnessing the search for truth and the exposure of injustice as a group of spectators places a corporate responsibility on the audience to acknowledge that injustice – and, potentially, to act to prevent similar future injustices. Third... there is a genuine hunger to engage with political material in a serious, unsensationalised manner... the stage is the perfect place to do so.[32]

Exercises for Part One

1. In class, try to come up with new ways of analysing verbatim theatre. You should at least think about whether you agree with our categories put forward in Chapter Two, and whether you find our 'spectrum' helpful when discussing these plays. Equally, you might not like our spectrum and might like to sketch a diagram or graph of your own. There is no single way of thinking about verbatim theatre.
2. At the end of Chapter Three, we raise a question about the potential of websites. This invites you to jump from the history of verbatim theatre to consider its possible futures. Discuss how the Internet might influence the development of documentary and verbatim theatre. Take a look at the on-line world of Second Life, and think about whether verbatim techniques have relevance there. What about mobile phones? As more and more material can be downloaded to phones, how may they be suited to documentary and verbatim theatre?
3. Clearly verbatim theatre has a past and a present, but even more exciting is its future. This is something to think about in the classroom, when making your own verbatim play or when performing one of the set plays. What do you like about the form? What do you dislike? What would you do differently? How could it be improved? What works on paper but fails on the stage? How would you feel if your story was told on stage? Who would you want to play you? Many contemporary verbatim plays have been developed in collaboration with students – think of Romaine Patterson and Jedadiah Schultz in *The Laramie Project*. Who knows, your play might be next.

Part Two

Plays in the Curriculum

Tara Morice, Mitchell Butel, Lynette Curran and Josef Ber in the 2001 Company B production of *The Laramie Project*. (Photo: Heidrun Löhr)

NSW Drama Curriculum
Topic 8: Verbatim Theatre

This topic explores, theoretically and experientially, plays written using the words of people interviewed about an issue or event and the social context, which gave rise to these plays. Students consider notions of authenticity and authority derived from direct testimony and community involvement. In particular, by engaging with the performance styles, techniques and conventions of the plays, students will explore the tension between maintaining truth while creating dramatic shape, theatricality and audience engagement.

TWO plays must be studied:
Compulsory text
- Kaufman, Moses, and Members of the Tectonic Theatre Project 2001, *The Laramie Project*, Vintage Books, Random House, New York.

AND EITHER
- Brown, Paul and Workers Cultural Action Committee 2001, *Aftershocks*, Currency Press, Sydney.

OR
- O'Connell, Terence 2004, *Minefields and Miniskirts*, Currency Press, Sydney.

OR
- Valentine, Alana 2007, *Parramatta Girls*, Currency Press, Sydney.

OR
- Valentine, Alana 2007, *Run Rabbit Run*, Currency Press, Sydney.

In the following chapters, you will find:
   a) notes on the play in context
   b) ideas for class discussions
   c) a guide to resources for further study

Throughout Part Two we also include comments from creative artists involved in Australian verbatim productions. These are extracts from interviews made by Roslyn Oades in late 2009. Full interviews and transcripts can be found on the Currency Press Verbatim website.

As you read the chapters relevant to the plays you have chosen to study, remember that the workshops in Part Three of this book are also designed to assist your exploration of the set curriculum plays. Teachers will also want to read Parts Two and Three in conjunction with: New South Wales Department of Education and Training, HSC Drama Prescriptions 2010–2012, Topic 8 verbatim theatre Teachers Notes, at www.curriculumsupport.education.nsw.gov.au/secondary/creativearts/assets/drama/pdf/verbatim.pdf

5.

The Laramie Project:

Performing the Play in the United States of America and Australia

CAROLINE WAKE

A) *THE PLAY IN CONTEXT*

On 7 October 1998, Matthew Shepard was found on the outskirts of Laramie, Wyoming, bound to a fence and beaten beyond recognition. The crime gained national attention and the town of Laramie found itself under intense scrutiny and sometimes under siege. On 19 February 2000, the Tectonic Theater Project premiered their play about this incident and its aftermath, *The Laramie Project*, at the Ricketson Theatre in Denver, Colorado. In the intervening sixteen months the company visited Laramie six times, carried out more than 200 interviews, and conducted five workshops. The result was a play that featured eight actors playing more than sixty characters and it was widely acclaimed; not only in Denver but also in New York and, finally, in Laramie itself.

Project development and production history in the United States

In retrospect, we can identify three stages in the play's development: interviewing, workshopping, and rehearsing. In reality, however, these stages often overlapped. For example, the company conducted its first round of interviews one month after Shepard's murder, in November 1998. When they conducted the first workshop in January 1999, they realised that they were missing some information and so, before their next workshop in April, some company members went back to Laramie in order to do additional interviews as well as to attend court hearings. In July, all twelve collaborators headed to the Sundance Theatre Lab, for a three-and-a-half week workshop. In August, the company did another workshop at Dartmouth College, sponsored by the New York Theatre Workshop, and by the end of this residency the first two acts had been 'roughed out'. The play still had no final act because the writers were waiting on the outcome of Aaron McKinney's trial in October 1999. When the company went into rehearsals in December 1999, they were still finalising the script.

> I think it was a very challenging piece. It's very long, it's almost three hours long, which is very long, and it held people's

attention for every moment. I think it's an extremely well-written play and I absolutely know that because the core at the heart of the structure is so powerfully strong and the story, it has been so well edited and so well shaped and crafted... I thought that there was something about the notion of the play that was about bearing witness to an event that the audience must make up their own minds about. Like, nobody knows what actually occurred before Matthew Shepard died and the play is actually asking you to examine your own prejudice at some level. Or to at least think about the way you conduct yourself in the world, if only briefly and that is maybe all we can hope for in this day and age.

Kate Gaul, director, 2001 Company B production of
The Laramie Project

The staging of verbatim plays is often minimalist. Photographs of the original *Laramie* production show a spare stage with wooden floors, several wooden chairs, and six screens – one large screen hanging upstage with five smaller, television-size screens hanging around it. Various images were projected onto the large screen throughout the performance. Often it was a sky; clear blue, sepia-tinted, or sometimes filled with grey clouds that seem to glow. Other times the screen was filled with the close-up of an actor's face. For example, during a media conference, the actor stood with his back to the audience while his face was filmed and projected onto the screen. In another scene, he faced the audience and his face was doubled, tripled, on the large screen above him and the smaller ones surrounding it. In amongst all of these faces, one remained noticeably absent: that of Matthew Shepard.

When the play premiered in Denver in February 2000, the Rocky Mountain News called it a 'riveting, thoughtful play' and when it transferred to off-Broadway in New York in May 2000, the response was similarly enthusiastic.[33] Most of the positive reviews are reproduced in the playscript. Although the critics' response was generally positive, it did attract the occasional criticism: one New York critic disliked the 'self-aggrandizing actors impersonating real folks'.[34] Nevertheless, when the company went back to Laramie in November 2000 to perform the play for the people they had interviewed, they received a two-minute standing ovation. By the end of the year 2000, the first production to be done without the original actors was underway in Florida and *Time Magazine* had listed *The Laramie Project* in its Top 10 Plays of the Year, describing it as a 'unique docudrama, constructed entirely from interviews with witnesses and participants. A pioneering work of theatrical reportage and a powerful stage event'.[35]

I had read the play three times and it was very moving at exactly the same times every time I read it so I was really sure that the machinery of the play was working. And on the basis of that I said I would do it. Because I knew it would be challenging, I had to be so sure about it in myself because I knew it would take a lot of... Verbatim plays of *The Laramie Project* nature are very difficult plays to rehearse and I needed to make sure that I had the energy and the commitment to it to keep a team of people on the project long enough for us to be able to get it in front of an audience with the joy and the spirit in which one should make theatre.

Kate Gaul

Production history in Australia

Three months later, in March 2001, *The Laramie Project* had its first production outside the United States with Company B at its Belvoir Street Theatre in Sydney. This production came about when set designer Brian Thomson saw the play on the final night of its New York run and called the company's Artistic Director, Neil Armfield, to recommend it. Once it had been programmed into their subscriptions season, Armfield offered it to Kate Gaul to direct. In order to direct the play, Kate Gaul went to New York to meet with the Tectonic Theater Project and then on to Laramie. While there, she spoke with some of the interviewees, as well as conducting additional interviews of her own. She also collected photographs, maps, newspaper clippings, tourist brochures, posters and postcards, all of which were eventually incorporated into the set on two long pin boards that framed the back walls of the stage. Hovering over all of this was a large photograph of Shepard. Perhaps the most complex problem facing the Australian production was the fact that the Australian actors would be playing the New York actors playing the Laramie residents. Despite contemplating a prologue to explain this, Moisés Kaufman of the Tectonic Theater Project and Gaul eventually decided against it.

When I came back from Laramie and I had lots and lots of research material, and of course the play's made up from a lot of research. We then decided to put in the pin boards and actually have the research materials as an extension of the actual stage and design. In fact, we had everything available to the audience but what actually happened from the day we did our first preview to the day we ended – and it was extraordinary in that it happened – is that people came into the theatre and they walked straight down onto the stage. There was no barrier. For some reason, whatever happened, there was no barrier between what was on the stage and the auditorium from the moment people walked into the theatre. That was an extraordinary experience in itself. Giving the audience that permission. They felt they had it, it wasn't anything that was planned. We had no idea that would happen. At interval people went straight down onto the stage and they did it at the end. I thought that that was really something, that was quite an event. [...] Oh yeah, we'd also decided, very early on in the design process to actually have a picture of Matthew Shepard as part of the design. That's not what they did in America because he was a well-known figure. So I thought that was a very... In Brian [Thomson]'s aesthetic, which I absolutely adore, is one very, very bold gesture. And so the giant-sized picture of Matthew Shepard, which would occupy the space as a sort of artefact in a way, was something that we went for.

Kate Gaul

It was really fascinating that as you were being told something, your eyes could just go across to this face and you could think, 'My god' as he was being hog-tied to the fence or this or that. And we decided that we would lean the photograph there and if we didn't think it was relevant, it would go. It wasn't part of the design, it was just brought in – it was huge. There was this sort of angelic face and just this sort of... the pain and the hurt and all that had happened.

Brian Thomson, designer, 2001 Company B production of The Laramie Project

For the most part, the response to Gaul's production of *The Laramie Project* was positive. Bryce Hallett of the *Sydney Morning Herald* described it as 'an absorbing, unexpectedly funny, honest and compassionate play'.[36] The *Sun Herald's* critic, Colin Rose, gave it 9/10, saying '[the play] speaks with rare power, by turns grim and affecting and, surprisingly, veined with humour'.[37] Not only did they like the play, they also liked its direction and especially its design. For instance, Hallett commented on the 'stark staging' and John McCallum described the set as 'simple and eloquent'.[38]

As with the United States production, the production did garner some criticism: McCarthy complained that 'one slightly irritating feature... [is] the intrusion of what in the media would be called personality journalism: the people reporting the story inevitably inject themselves into it as players in their own right'.[39] Similarly, Hallett noticed that the play had 'an unwieldy beginning' before it gained momentum. Colin Rose also said, 'It wouldn't be difficult to get the tone of this all wrong, to sound indignant, sentimental or smugly superior, and occasionally the play comes close to crossing the line'.[40] While Rose thought it came close to the line, Michael Bodey thought it actually crossed it, arguing 'There's a slight smugness about the latest Company B project, that doesn't sit comfortably with its harrowing subject matter'.[41]

Mitchell Butel in the 2001 Company B production of *The Laramie Project*. (Photo: Heidrun Löhr)

While some criticism centred on issues of staging or sentiment, others tended to focus on the issue of acting and authenticity. For instance, Bodey noted that 'The actors make varying work of the range of performances allowed... a couple of performers have trouble juggling character accents, some even juggling characters'.[42] Critic Carrie Kablean agreed that 'the American accents wobbled distractingly on opening night'.[43] Yet even when not focusing on the acting, issues of authenticity remained. Perhaps the most strident critic was playwright Nick Enright, who disliked that 'the irritating device of having the actors impersonate their American predecessors'. Referring to *The Simpsons*, he added it's like 'I'm actor Troy McClure, as it were, when we can see that the man addressing us is Australian actor Mitchell Butel'.[44]

For Enright, the play's resonance was 'weakened' by the fact that 'development ha[d] already been concluded', but for others the play was still socially relevant.[45] Philip McCarthy noted that the production coincided with the end of Mardi Gras, writing 'Ten days after the Sydney Gay and Lesbian Mardi Gras and its feel-good 2001 program of drag queens and cabaret artists, it is actually Neil Armfield's ostensibly mainstream theatre company that is filling the void for provocative content'.[46] Other participants argued that the play didn't need a particular point of connection with the Sydney community because the story is universal. For instance, actor Tara Morice commented that 'even beyond it being about Matthew Shepard and his case, it's a really universal piece because it's about prejudice and how people deal with violence'.[47]

> It's awful and profound, you know? Awful in a good way. There's some really sad stuff. Really sad. And the fact that it actually happened to someone and they had to live through that experience. I know when I have to tell big sad personal experiences it's really hard. I mean, you know that they've written it or they've said it in a blank moment, you know? It's not like they were planning on telling this story. There was no pretence when they offered their story. So it's kind of unguarded. You hear that in their stumbles and their choice of words. It's really sad. And it's beautiful – I think that's the thing – you don't get that in an imagined piece. Of course, there are brilliant writers that write amazing stuff that is heartbreaking as well. But, I don't know, I think it is just that mind-flick that makes you go, 'Wow! This is someone who lives and breathes in our time who has said this at some point and has had this as their history or their journey and that's profound – to step in their shoes as good as we can'.
>
> *Eliza Logan, actor, 2001 Company B production of*
> **The Laramie Project**

Though reviews provide us with a good idea of how the play was received, it's important to remember that there were other audience members whose responses go unrecorded. For example, one article in the *Daily Telegraph* mentions that 'a woman from Laramie, Wyoming, who knew Shepard, attended a performance and was quite emotional afterwards'.[48] In another article, Morice says that 'We had a group from a Victims of Crime organisation in for one of the preview performances and it was, of course, very personal for them'.[49] The responses to the play, published or otherwise, will always vary according to the audience members' background: a local resident of Laramie might respond in one way, a Sydney audience member who identifies as gay, lesbian, bisexual, transgender or queer might respond in another way, while someone without a personal connection to the material or the production will react differently again.

Shepard's mother, Judy, told a newspaper in Florida that she could not bring herself to sit and watch *The Laramie Project*, saying 'I've lived it and at this time don't feel I need to live it again. For others, it can be a valuable tool to understand and heal. I have heard nothing but rave reviews from my friends and family who have seen it. I know it is an important work'.[50]

Conclusion

When writing your essays, it might pay to specify which *Laramie Project* you're talking about: the published script; the productions in Denver, New York, and / or Laramie; the first production staged without the original actors in Florida; the first production in Sydney; or maybe a production staged by your school. The point is, the play isn't static, and it's going change depending on who is directing and acting in it, who's watching, and who's writing or talking about it.

> And with the part where [Matthew's] best friend, Romaine Patterson talks about the day that the protesters were there at the funeral... we theatricalised that quite a bit. We had surging singing going on sort of underneath that. I mean, theatrically you can build moments up as well. But that one, it wasn't an intimate kind of interview at all. I had to kind of basically shout above the sounds that were lifting and lifting on stage. That was a beautiful song, you know, a heartfelt rendition of 'Amazing Grace' or something incredibly... it was about rising up and joy. So in that respect, yes, again, I was telling everyone and occasionally pinpointed people [in the audience] but generally it was just like, 'Get this all of you!' So actually thinking of everybody as 'How cool was this?' I mean it was very sad but it was triumphant. And so in that respect you're thinking of the audience I guess as individuals who can all, kind of, possibly relate to this moment.

Eliza Logan

The Epilogue

The Laramie Project is ongoing. Ten years after the play's premiere, Tectonic Theater Project returned to Laramie to find out what had happened in the intervening years. The result was *The Laramie Project Epilogue*, an 80–minute performance staged simultaneously in 100 cities across the United States on 12 October 2009, by high schools, universities, professional regional theatres and, in New York, the original casts of the play and film. Webcasts and online interactive sessions accompanied the performance. On the same day in Australia, the Sydney University Dramatic Society performed the epilogue at the Seymour Centre.[51]

B) CLASS DISCUSSIONS

Authenticity

In the Company B production, the actors spoke with American accents but in the Sydney University production they didn't.
- What are the advantages and disadvantages of each approach?
- If you were directing the play, how would you have your actors speak? Why?

Acting

Tectonic Theater dramaturg Stephen Wangh has argued that there were a variety of acting styles at work in original production. He stated:

> Andy Paris was more interested than the other actors in gestural veracity, performing in the style Anna Deavere Smith. Other actors adhered to conventional acting, using their research to 'build' characters. Amanda Gronich was always a natural 'character' actor, doing vocal imitations, while Greg Pierotti made only slight personal adjustments in the direction of character.

- Do you think that one style of acting is more appropriate than another? If so, why?
- If you've seen the play in performance, how would you describe the acting styles in that production?
- If you haven't seen the play in performance, how you would direct actors in your own production?
- Which well known theatre practitioners would you refer to when describing the sort of acting style you prefer?

Staging

In the original production, Kaufman made a deliberate decision not to visually represent Matthew Shepard. In contrast, the Company B production featured a huge photograph of him.

- What are the advantages and disadvantages of each approach?
- What would you do if you were directing the play?

Social context and community

In the *Australian*, John McCallum said that 'A lot of people of Laramie are given a voice here, however filtered'.[52]

- In what ways do you think their voices are filtered and by whom?

For the Sydney production, Kate Gaul discussed the possibility of a prologue with Kaufman, but he declined to write one so she simply presented the play as it had been in Denver, New York, and Laramie. However, in an Adelaide production, the play started and finished with audio-taped observations on the 1972 drowning of a local homosexual man Dr George Duncan in order to give the play added local resonance.

- Do you think such a prologue is necessary or appropriate?
- If you were to devise a prologue for your community how would you go about it?
- What events or issues do you think you would include?

The Laramie Project Epilogue was performed on 12 October 2009 across the world.

- Conduct some research about how this was devised and received in the many simultaneous performances and via *The Laramie Project* web community.
- Return to the exercises on page 22, and revisit the question of how the Internet is influencing the development of verbatim theatre.

Dramatic shape

The current script of *The Laramie Project* has three narrative strands braided together: one about Shepard's time in Laramie; another about Laramie more generally and its response to the murder; and a third about the company's own experience in Laramie.

- Can you think of any stories that have been excluded?
- What else would you have liked to hear about?

In his introduction to the published play, Kaufman writes that the play has been created using what he calls 'moment work'. He defines a moment as 'a unit of theatrical time that is then juxtaposed with other units to convey meaning'.

- Can you think of other ways to structure the play? Could you, for instance, tell the story chronologically?
- Take some extracts from the play and rearrange the order. How does that order work? Is it better or worse and why?

Theatricality

In his introduction, Kaufman mentions Brecht's essay 'The Street Scene'.
- What do you think is Brechtian about the play?

In interviews, Kaufman also mentions his admiration for Meyerhold. When asked to describe a Meyerholdian moment, Kaufman suggests his staging of the arraignment (pp.44–5). He states: 'All the chairs are facing stairways, and as the court officer reads aloud the details of the crime, you see the bodies of the people listening slowly implode as the horror of the scene sinks in. That's the kind of reaction that can only be done onstage'.
- Can you think of other moments in the play that could become Meyerholdian?

Within the play itself, there are explicit references to Thorton Wilder's play *Our Town* as well as *Angels in America*.
- What do you know about these two plays?
- Why do you think Kaufman chose them as opposed to some others?

Don Shewey also drew parallels between companies such as the Living Newspaper, Max Stafford-Clark's Joint Stock Company, and Emily Mann's 'Theatre of Testimony'.
- What are the similarities and differences between the work of these companies and *The Laramie Project*?

Don Shewey also noted similarities between the work of the Wooster Group and the Tectonic Theater Project.
- What do you know about this company?
- How is its work similar to that of the Tectonic Theater Project?
- In what ways is it different?

Audience engagement

During the interval of the Company B production, spectators could go onto the stage to look at the set, which consisted of two pinboards covered in photographs, maps, newspaper clippings, tourist brochures, posters and postcards.
- What other methods could be used to increase audience involvement?

C) RESOURCES FOR FURTHER STUDY

Tectonic Theater Project

www.tectonictheaterproject.org/The_Laramie_Project.html
　　Here you can find original press coverage, along with a Teacher's Guide, a Student's Guide and numerous other features.

Tectonic Theater Project have also recently developed the online Laramie Project community: http://community.laramieproject.org/
This is also the best place to find information about *The Laramie Project Epilogue.*

Media coverage of Matthew Shepard's death

Thernstrom, Melanie. 'The Crucifixion of Matthew Shepard'. *Vanity Fair* (March 1999): 100–106, 145–153.

Wypijewski, JoAnn. 'A Boy's Life' *Harper's Magazine* (September 1999): 61–74.

Online resources

HBO Film: www.hbo.com/films/laramie
Time Magazine: www.time.com/time/classroom/laramie/
LiveJournal: community.livejournal.com/laramie_project/
Romaine Patterson: www.readromaine.com/site/index.html

Books about Laramie, Wyoming

Loffreda, Beth. *Losing Matt Shepard: Life and Politics in the Aftermath of Anti-Gay Murder.* New York: Columbia University Press 2000.

Academic articles

Baglia, Jay, and Elissa Foster. 'Performing the "Really" Real: Cultural Criticism, Representation, and Commodification in *The Laramie Project*'. *Journal of Dramatic Theory and Criticism* 19.2 (2005): 127–145.

Brown, Rich. 'Moisés Kaufman: The Copulation of Form and Content.' *Theatre Topics* 15.1: 51–67.

Claycomb, Ryan. '(Ch)oral History: Documentary Theatre, the Communal Subject and Progressive Politics' *Journal of Dramatic Theory and Criticism* (2003) 17.2: 95–121.

Dolan, Jill. 'The Laramie Project: Rehearsing for the Example'. *Utopia in Performance: Finding Hope at the Theater.* Ann Arbor: University of Michigan Press, (2005): 113–37.

Enright, Nick. 'Collaboration and Community: An Investigation into the Craft of the Actor and its Contribution to the Process of Making New Work for the Theatre'. *Rex Cramphorn Lecture 24* November 2002. www.currencyhouse.org.au/documents/ch_d_rex2002.pdf

Frommer, Martin Stephen. 'Thinking Relationally About Forgiveness: Commentary on Paper by Stephen Wangh'. *Psychoanalytic Dialogues* 15.1 (2005): 33–45.

Kiersky, Sandra M. 'Revenge and Forgiveness in Psychoanalysis: Commentary on Stephen Wangh's "Revenge and Forgiveness in Laramie, Wyoming"' *Psychoanalytic Dialogues* 15.5 (2005): 771–778.

Sandage, Stephen J. 'Intersubjectivity and the Many Faces of Forgiveness'. *Psychoanalytic Dialogues* 15.1 (2005): 17–32.
Tigner, Amy. 'The Laramie Project: Western Pastoral'. *Modern Drama* 45.1 (2002): 138–156.
Wangh, Stephen. 'Revenge and Forgiveness in Laramie, Wyoming'. *Psychoanalytic Dialogues* 15.1 (2005): 1–16.
Wangh, Stephen. 'Reply to Commentaries' *Psychoanalytic Dialogues* (2005) 15.1: 47–56.

6.

Aftershocks:

Voices from a Shaken Community

MEG MUMFORD

A) *THE PLAY IN CONTEXT*

At 10.27am on 28 December 1989, the Australian city of Newcastle was hit by an earthquake measuring 5.6 on the Richter scale. As well as damaging over 50,000 buildings in central-eastern NSW, the quake took the lives of thirteen people, nine of whom died in the Newcastle Workers Club when its concrete and steel structure plummeted into the ground floor car park.[53] After the event, facts such as these, as well as the opinions of official experts and footage of visiting politicians, were duly transmitted through an array of mass media forms. On some occasions, the transmission process had its own fault lines, such as when international television erroneously presented neighbouring Sydney, Australia's commercial and tourism hub, as the site at the heart of the quake.

Many Novocastrians, especially those connected in some way with the Club, were even more dissatisfied with the lack of media attention to the knowledge and expertise, heroism and aftermath experiences of everyday working people. Such errors and omissions are not uncommon in a public domain dominated by the point of view of busy journalists under considerable pressure to create brief and catchy stories in a very short period of time. First performed on 12 November 1991, after an intensive research and development period, one of the aims of *Aftershocks* was to provide an alternative to the ways such a media system creates and communicates understandings of social crisis.

Australian community theatre meets verbatim drama

Aftershocks was the product of collaboration between a number of participants with close personal connections to the Club. One of these contributors was the Workers Cultural Action Committee (WCAC), a subcommittee of the Newcastle Trades Hall whose premises were (and still are) part of the Club, and which fosters cultural development among local workers and their families. The Committee contributed to the research, development and production of both the theatre and 1998 film versions. They were joined by many affiliates, including: the Club historian and board member, Bob Phillips, whose raw and moving interviews with people directly after the quake provided inspiration and materials for the script; and by staff and students from the University of Newcastle, including community theatre scholar David Watt who had a dramaturgical role in the project and co-directed the first production of *Aftershocks* with Brent McGregor, then Director of the Hunter Valley Theatre Company. A steering committee of trade unionists and Club personnel became project advisors.

> The most important initial thing that happened was Bob Phillips interviewing people about the earthquake within two weeks of it happening. So there he was with a tape recorder – high quality gear – going 'round to people that he knew, the workers in the Club, the patrons of the Club, who'd been affected by the earthquake. I'm not sure he had clear ideas about what would become of the material but just as the Workers Cultural Action Committee knew something had to be done, Bob Phillips, as a historian, knew that he had to respond, he had to ask people about this. So he conducted this oral history project... When you go back to them, they have quite a different quality to the interviews that we ended up doing a whole year later... By the time you get to the following January, which is when we did a lot of our research for the play and many of the interviews, the interviews we were getting had been processed through that whole year of telling and retelling the story.
>
> ***Paul Brown, playwright,* Aftershocks**

At his first meeting with the project's steering committee in November 1990, Brown presented the option of a ritualised and large-scale community piece that would be staged on the Club site.[54] However, due to the steering group's interest in a more enduring and transportable artwork, one that would tour the 'unofficial' stories of primary witnesses far and wide, the project headed instead towards a collectively devised and publishable play that could be performed by a small cast in a variety of venues. Brown took on the roles of research facilitator, lead editor of the transcript material, and key creator of the play's structure. The decision to use testimonials from people connected with the Club to help build the actors' speeches was in keeping with community theatre's participatory agenda. However, the decision to create a verbatim drama based entirely on (only minimally) edited transcripts – what Brown has termed 'pure' verbatim – was a bold new departure for this field of Australian theatre.

The collaborators' use of verbatim methods was influenced by their familiarity both with community projects based on oral history techniques, and with British and Canadian verbatim drama. What determined their commitment to a 'pure' verbatim text, however, was firstly the power of the transcript narratives from Bob Phillips' initial interviews, particularly the poetry and verve of the vernacular language which also provided a distinctive 'voiceprint' for every character. Secondly, it was agreed that an approach to text that emphasised fidelity to the interviewees' words and ways of speaking was a valuable strategy for ensuring that marginalised voices would be heard and given authority, and that interviewees retained control over their stories.[55]

Eight researchers, all connected with the Club community, conducted and transcribed twenty-three new interviews made one year after the quake, with the researchers often paired with interviewees who were workmates or friends. There was further community input via feedback mechanisms: the researchers performed a reading of the first draft in early February 1991 before an audience that included the interviewees, steering group, WCAC, theatre workers, and university students and staff. On the basis of this feedback, the authors committed themselves to a stripped-back production focused on the art of storytelling, and a greater centralisation of the Club's history and its significance for the workers and patrons.

It is likely that the commitment to both textual fidelity and community connectedness contributed to the vivid and intimate nature of the interviewees' responses. One particularly detailed interview was that between David Owen, a cleaner at the Club, and John Constable, another cleaner who became a rescuer during the quake and one of the main characters in the play. Locked away in the Newcastle Trades Hall kitchen for around three hours, both men discussed the details of the collapse while poring over the plans of the Club, with Constable explaining exactly where he went within the precarious ruins of the building. This interview, and Owen's creative decision to use the map, not only made an important contribution to the structure and action of the play, but also exemplified collaborative authorship throughout the play-making process. The kitchen interview also enhanced the play's acknowledgment of the Club workers' daily routines and associated local knowledge, a type of knowledge neglected in media coverage and relatively downplayed in the 1998 film version (where much of the play's opening text about the nature of the characters' work activities within the Club was removed). In Brown's eyes, a contributing factor for Constable's two successful rescue operations was his familiarity with the building and the location of colleagues and patrons within it.[56]

> John is a fabulously flawed hero. In every classic sense of the drama because he was a very popular person but he had a streak of irresponsibility about him that had got him into trouble. There's a speech where he talks about Lyn, who was his supervisor at the Club, treating him a bit like a son. She was obviously mentoring him, trying to get him on track, so to speak. If you like, it gives you the B-Story: 'John's Personal

Journey and His Relationship With Lyn'. And that he ends up rescuing her is just a gold nugget that you're always looking for in verbatim work where it's very unpredictable. But you do keep your antennae up looking for things like that which are so strong dramatically that you know they're going to be in and you know that they're going to help with the structure.

Paul Brown

Artistic negotiation towards a truth

The play's attention to work expertise, and to a building and site associated with unionism, is an example of what Brown has called verbatim theatre's 'negotiation towards a truth'.[57] While *Aftershocks* may seem like 'the' truth, it remains only one truth and the construct of a particular process.[58] In this case the process was shaped by the authors' interests in the following five main subject areas and themes:

1) insider perspectives on the quake, rescue management and communication;
2) the economic, social and psychological impact as experienced in the aftermath;
3) authority on the day of the quake and story ownership;
4) the identity and social significance of the Club;
5) the ongoing struggle to deal with negative and chaotic experience.[59]

The team's focus on working life, unofficial stories, local knowledges, authority structures, the idea of 'club' and its community, and the management of crisis greatly influenced the content and structure of the interviews and subsequently the play itself.

A structure of vivid grabs and nodal scenes

Aftershocks was also shaped by a desire to create an entertaining and enduring drama, both about the Club and the responses to natural disaster. To this end, Brown used a number of editorial and artistic strategies to create scenes. He first broke down transcripts into discreet story fragments – what he refers to in filmic terms as 'grabs' – to be combined and shaped in search of scenes that would be memorably illustrative of key events and themes. The creation of distilled narratives involved an erasure of the traces of the event that had generated them, the real life interview. As Brown writes: 'The "ums", "ahs", "you knows" and other words which were there only because of the interview process itself were mostly edited out'.[60] The questions and responses of the interviewer were also removed, and the fact that most of the research participants were interviewed alone rather than in pairs or groups (with the exception of the couples Howard and Elaine Gibson and

Gillian Jones, Jacqui Phillips, John Jarratt and Jeremy Sims in the 1993 Company B production of *Aftershocks*. (Photo: Paul Wright)

Fay and Bob Asquith) was lost in the many multiple-character scenes that interwove 'grabs' from a variety of interviews.

The juxtaposition and interweaving of discreet story fragments was one of the main methods for creating a scene. For example, parts of the solo interviews with bar attendant, Kerry Ingram, and her friend, Marg Turnbull, from the poker machine area, were merged together to create moments such as 'Scene Sixteen – Adrenalin':

> **KERRY:** Once the ambulance arrived, they threw bandages and whatever else at us, you know, anybody who knew how to tie a bandage was in.
> **MARG:** And people came from everywhere with jugs of water, and cups and things. They were washing people's mouths out, and washing their eyes out, and whatever...
> **KERRY:** And yet there was... there was other people standing around just looking. Able-bodied men who were letting women carry other men, and you felt like grabbing some of them and shaking the hell out of them and saying, 'Get in there and do something', because the management and that, they wouldn't let the women back in.[61]

This scene exemplifies Brown's interest in finding what he calls 'nodes', moments of intersection between separate stories where the speakers address the same subject matter from different or complementary perspectives. Such scenes also explore the role of lay expertise in a crisis situation, and of the way the heroes and heroines of the day were often not the socially sanctioned or official figures of authority.

Storytellers and their community of witnesses

One of the intriguing features of all the playtext scenes, especially those involving multiple characters, is the way they invite actors to become storytellers and witnesses rather than mimics of real life interviewees and (verbal) dialogue partners. As mentioned above, *Aftershocks* does not seek to verbally imitate the original interviews upon which it is based. Rather, as the following note from the First Edition of the script about the Brechtian technique of having actors announce scene titles testifies, the text encourages a self-conscious storytelling approach:

> *Note: This convention of captioning scenes was adopted by the Newcastle cast. It is one way for the actors to confirm that they are primarily storytellers rather than the characters themselves.[62]

In the Newcastle production of 1991, the play's status as an artistic construct was foregrounded by the listing of the scene titles on the back wall, and their announcement directly to the audience. The decision to use role doubling in the Newcastle show (with six actors playing sixteen characters), and the manipulation of gestures, blocking and props to help convey the stories, further underscored the fact that far from being 'the' truth about the quake, this drama was 'one' truth, constructed through a process of combining (but not seamlessly joining) the words of primary witnesses with the work of interpreters and entertainers. To some extent, the impact of the difference between interviewee and actor was lost in the 1998 film where the type casting, with each actor only playing one character, reduced the display of the performers and their storytelling skills.

The use of sparse and metonymic props and setting in the first productions, and indeed in the many that have followed, further underlines its status as a constructed telling of the story. Take, for example, the use of chairs in the Newcastle production. These simple objects were used by the actors to play out bits of the narratives. They moved chairs around the space in different configurations to show the literal and figurative decimation of the Club, and to construct 'safe' storytelling spaces on the stage.[63] (In real life, during the quake the large number of chairs housed in the building were flung in every direction.) In the Belvoir Street Theatre production the design of the floor-to-ceiling stacks of red, plastic chairs up against the back wall prompted reviewer Angela Bennie to sense 'a movement through the chairs, like a shiver and a shudder – a subtle, clever and disturbing visual sign of the equivocal nature of the world surrounding us'.[64]

> We were going to do it with all projection and we were going to tell the entire story visually as well as through the play. And then we realised – I think it might have even happened after the first read through – I just thought, 'This is just not right at all'. And then essentially we pretty much took what was in rehearsal and put it in a theatre. And I think we did one wall... There's one of those stackable orange chairs, we had one wall of those from the floor to the ceiling and people who saw the play were convinced that they moved. And they didn't. It was just the way when you stack up that many chairs and go as high as you can, we had to kind of like tie them to the wall, you get a certain rhythm happening in it and people believed that we shook them but that didn't happen.
>
> **Brian Thomson, designer, 1993 Company B production of Aftershocks**

In *Aftershocks*, the storyteller-actors' acknowledgment of their artistic labour could be described as Brechtian. However, unlike the epic actor, their focus is on listening to the character's point of view, and testifying on their behalf, rather than on providing a distancing commentary about the character's social significance. In verbatim theatre productions, particularly those concerning traumatic events, the empathetic listening to characters that the plays encourage from actors and spectators is often modelled by the onstage ensemble of actors. It is common in such theatre for those actors who are not involved in a particular scene to remain on stage and be choreographed as a group of witnesses who respond to each character as they speak. This may involve, say, clustering around in sympathy, or bringing in a chair for a speaker to sit on prior to a tough moment in the story. Such choreography replaces dialogue with what Brown calls 'shared witness'.[65] In this kind of staging, one primary witness of a traumatic event seems to listen to and testify in the presence of another. At the same time, a multitude of other (secondary) witnesses are present, including other onstage ensemble members, and the audience, any one of whom may or may not have themselves directly experienced the traumatic event or testimonies about it. Unlike Brecht's theatre of contradiction, where oppositional relationships between characters, performers and spectators are established in order to generate new insights, *Aftershocks* is a type of testimonial theatre which places emphasis on creating a community of empathetic listeners who share the task of bearing witness.

Just a local story?

As the authors had hoped, many audiences across Australia have witnessed the unofficial story of *Aftershocks*, which has now been performed in most of the nation's states and in a diverse range of school, university, community theatre and professional mainstream contexts.[66] A telemovie version directed by Geoff Burton was screened by SBS on 29 December 1998, which garnered further national attention when Jeremy Sims received an Australian Film Industry Award for his portrayal of John Constable. While much community drama has a relatively brief life span, precisely because it is devised to meet the needs of a group in a particular time and place, *Aftershocks* continues to be read and performed. One of the reasons for its relatively enduring nature is no doubt its careful attention to a social crisis brought about by a natural disaster, a source of crisis that continues to be feared across the globe.

However, the reception of the play's material has raised some interesting issues about whether, and if so how, an interpretation or performance of the work can balance its commitment to, on the one hand, the specific experience and knowledge of a local community, and on the other hand, its exploration of more broadly relevant issues. In his review of the 1995 Melbourne Theatre Company production, Guy Rundle concludes that the play lacks relevance for a non-local and historically removed audience, and attributes this to the comparatively small-scale nature of the traumatic event, as well as the community drama genre:

> ... at this remove of time and space, the deep and searching examination of the psychological effects of the event, seem almost excessive, a sort of community theatre meets *Oprah*. Compared to the daily bulletins from Bosnia, an earthquake, as far as disasters go, is practically a benign event... Community theatre rarely travels well.

Because it is a community speaking to itself about itself, and breaking down the distinction between producers and consumers of culture, to be successful it must not only be local but must also avoid the artistic synthesis plot, patterning, symbol that makes particular material of general appeal. Out of context, its freshness becomes shapelessness, its localism, parochialism.[67]

By contrast, in her review of the 1993 Belvoir Street Theatre performance, Angela Bennie concludes that under Neil Armfield's direction:

Newcastle's story becomes our story, everyone's story.... *Aftershocks* becomes a tribute to human decency, courage and endurance. It is a testimony to our love and need for each other, our families and friends. It is a testimony to our capability for the unselfish act, the generous gesture without reward. It bears witness to our need for some kind of moral order, to the notion that altruisim is just as important a human characteristic as is individualism.[68]

A similar emphasis on the universal relevance of the play's material can be found in Elisabeth Wynhausen's review of the same production, where she describes the play as coming 'closer than one might have thought possible to looking into the heads and hearts of ordinary, decent Australians trying to cope with catastrophe'.[69]

Newcastle actor Paul Makeham, who was a member of the research team and a performer in the first production, has criticised the universalist responses to the Belvoir show for reducing the Newcastle Workers Club to an 'Everyclub' stereotype, and particular individuals to 'emblematic "human-in-crisis" figures'. He argues that the universalist paradigm effaces 'those differences – of locale, class, experience and so on' which exist between non-local audiences and the characters of the play.[70] It could be added that such an approach is deeply at odds with community verbatim theatre's interest in airing different and marginalised voices. While Makeham affirms the importance of local specificity to the political potential of the play, unlike Rundle he does not agree that this means the play will lack relevance when it travels beyond its founding community. Rather, in a Brechtian manner, he exhorts reader-spectators (and by implication, theatre-makers as well) to become more willing to engage with the people, languages and spaces of unfamiliar social worlds. As the reception of *Aftershocks* makes clear, one of the major challenges for anyone interested in performing the play or in making a similarly mobile and enduring work, is to ensure that neither parochialism nor universalism usurp its engagement with a community of local voices.

B) CLASS DISCUSSION TOPICS AND EXERCISES

Historical fact meets fiction: performing a local story away from home

The authors of *Aftershocks* were eager from the very start that the play would be performed by people and in locations outside the Newcastle community it depicts. In an interview with Roslyn Oades, Brown stated that the script should be treated like any other, which means that those who wish to produce it can choose how they are going to interpret and stage characters, events and settings. He believes that the script encourages research into, for example, the history of the quake and why the play was written, as well as the living or historical interviewees.

- If you were to direct or act in a production of *Aftershocks*, what approach towards the information and evidence about the quake and its survivors would you take and why?
- Would you try to generate more information, for example by contacting the survivors or any of the other authors?
- In preparing a scene for performance, see what emerges if half of your class conducts research alongside analysing the text, while the other half just analyses the text. Then each group's performance of the same scene could be compared and discussed.

Dramatic shape: monologues and nodal scenes

In *Aftershocks* (as in most verbatim plays), monologues are combined into nodal scenes which interweave fragments from different interviewee speeches. The end result is something akin to, but distinct from, dialogue, with characters seeming at once isolated and even lonely, and yet connected with a community of listeners.

- What are some of the differences in process between interviewing one person and doing group interviews? How does the material generated differ?
- In what circumstances might one of these interview methods be preferable?
- When it comes to making scenes, how does the exclusion or inclusion of the interviewer change the content, form, meaning and audiences' experience of a play?
- Experiment in class with different ways to make interviews and different ways to incorporate them into scenes.

Acting conventions: imitation, storytelling, commentary

In her 1993 review of the Belvoir Street Theatre production of *Aftershocks*, Angela Bennie rhetorically asks why the material should be performed in the theatre: 'Why not just film the people giving their testimonies and keep this as the people's record of this terrible event?'

- How would you answer Bennie's question?
- Address this issue by considering how such material can be performed in the theatre, and the types of ideas and experiences that different performance methods can generate.
- Use interview material gathered by the class to experiment with the impact of different performance methods. The first could be an accurate imitation of the bodies, voices, language and location of the interviewer and interviewee, that is, an attempt to reconstruct the interview. The second could be using storyteller–actors, each of whom play more than one character, directly addressing the audience, and working with minimal set and props. You could also trial the 'headphone-verbatim' technique described by Roslyn Oades (see Chapter 11: Creating a Headphone-Verbatim Performance).

C) **RESOURCES FOR FURTHER STUDY**

Books and articles

Anderson, Michael and Linden Wilkinson. 'A Resurgence of Verbatim Theatre: Authenticity, Empathy and Transformation' *Australasian Drama Studies* 50 (2007): 153–69.

Brown, Paul. '*Aftershocks*: Local Stories, National Culture' *Meanjin* 54, 3 (1995): 449–60.

Brown, Paul. '*Aftershocks*: Verbatim Theatre About the 1989 Newcastle Earthquake: A Work in Progress' *Oral History Association of Australia Journal* 13 (1991): 49–55.

Brown, Paul and Workers Cultural Action Committee, *Aftershocks*. Sydney: Currency Press, second edition 2001. (This edition contains an introduction: '*Aftershocks*: Ten Years in the Making' which, among other things, describes how the play became a film.)

Makeham, Paul. 'Community Stories: *Aftershocks* and Verbatim Theatre' *Our Australian Theatre in the 1990s* Ed. Veronica Kelly. Amsterdam and Atlanta: Rodopi (1998): pp.168–81.

Makeham, Paul. 'Interview' *Dramactive* (Book 2) Eds. Madonna Stinson and Debbie Wall. North Ryde, NSW: McGraw-Hill, (2005), pp.73–6.

Phillips, Bob. *The Red Inn: The First 50 Years of Newcastle Workers Club* Newcastle: Newcastle Workers Co-operative Club 1998.

Play reviews

Bennie, Angela. 'Courage Triumphs Amid the Chaos' *The Sydney Morning Herald* 15 July 1993 p.17.

Burchall, Greg. 'Earthquake Drama is Theatre Verbatim' *The Age* 24 July 1995 p.20.
Carroll, Steven. 'Reliving an Earth-shattering Experience' *The Sunday Age* 30 July 1995 p.7.
Longworth, Ken. 'No Cracks Appearing Here' *The Newcastle Herald* 16 September 2002 p.50.
Mansfield, Garry. 'Quake of Fear: *Aftershocks*' *Sun Herald* 29 December 1998 p.71.
Morgan, Joyce. 'Up the Workers, Up on Stage' *The Sydney Morning Herald* 23 August 1999 p.13.
Payne, Pamela. 'Fault Lines' *The Sydney Morning Herald* 12 July 1993 p.22.
Payne, Pamela. 'Newcastle Earthquake Revisited' *Sun Herald* 25 July 1993 p.135.
Pennels, Steve. 'Survivors Tell of Horror Quake' *The West Australian* 29 December 1998, p.5.
Rundle, Guy. 'Tragedy Told Simply' *The Age* 28 July 1995 p.19.
Wynhausen, Elisabeth. 'Newcastle Quake Hits the Stage' *Sun Herald* 25 July 1993 p.38.

Television adaptation

Aftershocks. Dir. Geoff Burton. Australia: Ronin Films 1998.

Television reviews

Everton, Denise. 'Television' *Illawarra Mercury* 29 December 1998 p.47.
Gripper, Ali. 'After Shocks' *The Sydney Morning Herald* 28 December 1998 p.4.
Johnston, Tony. 'Disaster that Shook a Nation' *Sunday Herald Sun* 27 December 1998 p.5.
Joyce, James. 'Story of Survival' *Newcastle Herald* 15 August 1998 p.6.
McDonald, Patrick. 'After the Shock' *Adelaide Advertiser* 23 December 1998 p.49.
Williams, Sue. 'No Thanks for Quake Memory' *Sun Herald* 29 November 1998 p.21.

Website

www.ausstage.edu.au/advancedsearchresult.jsp?xcid=135 (AusStage database on *Aftershocks* productions)

7.

Minefields and Miniskirts:

Women's Voices and the Vietnam War

Paul Brown

A) **THE PLAY IN CONTEXT**

More so than any of the other set plays, *Minefields and Miniskirts* lends itself to a study of the link between personal stories and major transformations in the history of modern Australia. Writing in the *Oxford Companion to Australian History*, John Murphy describes the Vietnam War as:

> The longest and most divisive of Australia's military engagements. For a decade from 1962, Australian forces were involved in a complex conflict which was in part civil war [between North and South Vietnam], and in part a proxy conflict in the Cold War. These complexities generated intense dispute in Australia, and are reflected in divisions in the historical literature.[71]

In studying *Minefields and Miniskirts*, we must take into account the marked impact the Vietnam War had on individuals and the Australian society as a whole. But we should also remain mindful of the disagreement about how to record and write the history of the war, which Murphy mentions above. The play is an adaptation of an important contribution to that recorded history, a compilation of interviews made by oral historian Siobhan McHugh, in her 1993 book of the same name. Her focus is on the role and experience of women in the Vietnam War, a dimension largely ignored in most other prominent historical analyses.

> I think the oral historian records the lived experiences of their interviewee and seeks to understand and to hear a life story... somebody's very personal life story. There's a very personal element to oral history. It's part of the whole fabric of oral history interviews: that you don't shy away from the intimate details. So you want to gather material on what somebody did but also the context in which they did it and how they feel now about what happened to them. So you're gathering the emotional memory and the emotional truth as well as the nuts and bolts of whatever you're interviewing them about... [First you] explore with as much authenticity and depth as you

can... I find the biggest thing is if people feel like they're really being heard they'll open up. And that of course involves a lot of trust... and then you are the bearer of that story and, your second task, is how do you convey it, pass it on, in such a way that it retains a real sense of who they are. But you inevitably, because of the medium, have to distil it or edit it or be selective. It's how to be selective without misrepresenting that I think is the great responsibility of the oral historian.

Siobhan McHugh, author, **Minefields and Miniskirts**

Most living Australians born before 1955 will have strong recollections of the Vietnam War. From 1964 to 1972, all males turning twenty had to register for 'National Service'. Military conscription had previously divided Australians, but this was the first time conscripts could be sent overseas to a war zone. The possibility of young men being selected by ballot to fight meant that in almost all families, the war had an impact directly and personally. Conscription became a point of intense debate inside families, in the media, in the political arena, and, ultimately, in the streets.

Conscription was not the only focus of political debate about the Vietnam War. There were questions about whether the war was justified, since to many Australians the so-called 'Communist threat' from China via North Vietnam seemed to lack substance; and there was disagreement about whether Australia should follow the United States into such a war. The new technologies of war (such as incendiary bombs and the use of defoliating chemicals) entrapped Vietnamese people, whether military or civilian, in a brutal conflict played out in rice paddies and villages. Meanwhile, the military personnel involved seemed psychologically unprepared for the atrocities of the battlefields and guerilla war zones which they witnessed or themselves perpetrated. These atrocities were graphically covered in the media, which had unprecedented access and, through television, a new-found ability to easily communicate the stories and images of the war across the world.

The 1960s saw the worldwide rise of new social movements, determined to confront governments on civil and indigenous rights, feminism, the environment, labour relations, nuclear threats, and war and conscription. By about 1968, there was growing support for an anti-war campaign, involving street marches of protestors calling for a Moratorium on the war and an end to conscription. Australia began to withdraw its troops in 1970, and when the Labor government was elected in 1972, Prime Minister Gough Whitlam ordered all remaining troops home and abolished conscription.[72]

By that time, so strong was the anti-war sentiment among a majority of Australians, that many of those who had participated in the war, whether as volunteer troops or as conscripts, returned home to open criticism from protestors, and returned veterans often chose to conceal their participation in the war. In some ways, they became an invisible cohort, doubly disadvantaged as the after-effects of exposure to battlefield chemicals or psychological trauma began to emerge as health and family problems. Kept even further out of view were the experiences of women in the Vietnam War. Yet, as *Minefields and Miniskirts* portrays, they participated as nurses, observers, journalists, entertainers, and as the wives, mothers and sisters of servicemen. The Vietnam War continues to impact the lives of veterans and their families, and women in several respects go on making some of the most enduring and significant contributions as this major piece of Australian history unfolds.

> I went and interviewed two nurses, just as a pilot to see. And just the descriptions they gave of the Vietnam War were so different from anything I'd ever heard. I'd seen all the movies that were out at that time and it was an entirely male, militaristic view. Vietnam was a war to the men but to the women, Vietnam was a culture, a place, a people, a country. The issues they talked about were very personal, very emotional, there was a lot of humour, there was a lot of sadness. I realised they were talking in a way we hadn't heard so I started to explore; to move it out − 'What other kinds of women were there?' Well, there were civilian nurses as well, there were journalists, there were entertainers, there were all kinds of secretarial staff, and then there were miscellaneous women who found themselves there working at the embassy or with husbands or whatever. I decided to make the female views of the Vietnam War.
>
> *Siobhan McHugh*

Apart from the war itself, there is a key Australian event that gave impetus to *Minefields and Miniskirts*. On 3 October 1987, some 25,000 people who had participated in the Vietnam War marched through the streets of Sydney, in what was known as 'The Welcome Home March'. The march was the most visible element of reconciliation between those who opposed the war and those who fought, and of a new public understanding of the Vietnam War, controversial though it remains. As it became easier for all Australians to converse about the war, both in public and within families, new histories emerged, including women's history. Siobhan McHugh's book is a highly-valued contribution, in the oral history tradition, to these processes of reconciliation and a new understanding of Australia's past.

History of the play

All verbatim plays could be described as 'adaptations' of other material, most commonly the transcripts of interviews. But *Minefields and Miniskirts* is distinct from the other set curriculum plays because its playscript was adapted from McHugh's previously published book, which emerged more than a decade before Terence O'Connell acquired the rights to make his adaptation for the stage.[73] McHugh and O'Connell agree that in the finished play, about ninety percent of the language is derived from the book, with the remainder being O'Connell's adaptation and invention. The most important change is that the play presents five 'composite' characters whose speeches are derived from a much larger number of women originally interviewed by McHugh. In this way, *Minefields and Miniskirts* resembles Alana Valentine's *Parramatta Girls*. (See Chapter 8 *Parramatta Girls*: Verbatim Theatre about the Forgotten Australians.)

Another interesting aspect of the *Minefields and Miniskirts* process was that McHugh initially faced the problem that the 'community' of women involved with the Vietnam War is dispersed and generally not well networked (though today there are important remedies to this, such as the Veterans Wives Group website). To overcome this, she began her search for stories with an open advertisement in newspapers and on community radio. The stories of her early interviewees suggested groups of women who could be involved, and McHugh's contacts then extended to musicians' unions and groups of civilian nurses. Approximately half of the fifty interviews were conducted with women who went to Vietnam; the other half of the interviews covered the equally rich experiences of wives and widows of Vietnam veterans, from which emerged the theme of women who cope with their husbands' post-traumatic stress.

> I got onto that idea that the wives had coped with the emotional burden of the traumatised veterans and that led me to interview civilian wives over here who'd stayed at home. I found that remarkably strong. That side had never been explored at that time. What struck me very forcefully about that was that was a story that was common to all wars... you know, shell shock, battle fatigue, whatever you call it... people going through extraordinary and awful times and then being psychologically disturbed as a result and reliving them to some degree or another when they came back... Every single wife I interviewed would talk about 'walking on eggshells' – they used that phrase – tip-toeing around the husband in case he would erupt. Something would trigger an outburst and it would be either that rage or some kind of violence, either physical or emotional violence.
>
> *Siobhan McHugh*

After being strongly influenced by a major museum exhibition about the Vietnam War, theatre workers Terence O'Donnell and Ken Moffat approached Siobhan McHugh with a view to adaptation for the stage. Although McHugh was cautious, she was quickly convinced that the work's integrity would be retained. After a year of discussion and another year of play development by Terence O'Connell, *Minefields and Miniskirts* premiered in July 2004 for Melbourne's C.U.B. Playbox Theatre at the Malthouse. The play was very well received in its initial season and went on to tour extensively in both metropolitan and regional Australia.

We will conclude this section with extracts from Roslyn Oades' interviews with Siobhan McHugh and Terence O'Connell, in which they discuss the process of adaptation for the stage and the impact of the play. You could read these in conjunction with Siobhan McHugh's paper on the 'pleasures and perils of adapting oral history for the stage'.[74]

TERENCE O'CONNELL: Well, I can't remember what year this was maybe 2002 or 3, there was a huge exhibition at the Melbourne Museum about Australians in the Vietnam War which included footage and uniforms and flags and photographs and costumes from entertainers who went there. It was remarkable. And so I saw that and I went to see it a few times... Then I think the following year, someone rang me up and said, 'I've just read this book, you should do a show from this book'. So we started to negotiate with Siobhan to get the rights to adapt it for theatre.

SIOBHAN MCHUGH: I think it was because the oral history was so live on the page, that the theatrical potential was apparent. My big interest was, when I met Ken, to be sure that they had the right attitude. In other words, they were aligned. They weren't going to misrepresent the women's stories or stitch them up. I was terrified that somebody could just make a grab bag out of quotes and take things out of context and distort the reality of what the women had told me. My duty to the women is that their story be told as authentically and as interestingly as possible.

TERENCE: Once we had got the rights from Siobhan for the book and all the legals had been sorted then it was, 'Oh, how to do it'. The thing that struck me most as an image or an idea was... almost all of these women said when they hear a helicopter it takes them back there. So that idea was how I decided to start the show so you would see them at... 'The Welcome Home March' as it was called, and as a helicopter goes over, they join in a sort of shared memory of the events, then enter this world of shared imagination. The women wore Asian-style clothing with Australian emblems on them and it was set in an extraordinary bamboo tea room, house of the imagination. Again it was showing you somehow that a good part of these women's hearts and minds were still in that country at that time and, indeed, still are... I decided to use songs from the period... that floated through the evening. A lot of it was underscored by a sort of contemporary Asian soundtrack as well.

ROSLYN: So the form and the design unlocked it for you?

TERENCE: Yeah, it did. Once we had that and the interviews it was, 'Well, that woman's story very is interesting but it finishes too early' or 'That woman's story, that's a great bit but it's repetitive of another woman's story'. That was the interesting bit of trying to edit and trying to give them a through-line. Some of which I invented, especially early on [in the play] and towards the end as well. Events were invented or exaggerated or made clearer. But it's certainly totally stuck to the spirit and largely the letter of the book.

ROSLYN: So once you found five characters, or five personalities, you were able to then attribute stories that would be believable for them to experience?

TERENCE: That's right, or move some of the stories around because it felt better for this woman to have this rather than this... Siobhan totally trusted us in the end and didn't come to any rehearsal or anything and just came for the first time on the opening night.

SIOBHAN: I saw the first night in Melbourne at the Malthouse in 2004 and I saw the play script the day it opened. That was the first time I saw it. So I had completely handed it over as an artistic process and it was very scary because if he'd got it 'wrong': if he'd made a complete pig's arse of the characters, it would have been mortifying for everybody. It would have been mortifying for the women, it would have been mortifying for me, and it probably wouldn't have worked as a play.

ROSLYN: Do you think the integrity of the work is still there?

SIOBHAN: Yeah, I do very much. First of all the notion of the composite character, the nurse's story, it blends with some of the civilian experiences with some of the military women but, each of them was looking after a patient and had a story about that... He kind of ad libbed a bit... [As one example] the bit about the Chinese restaurant, that sentence is one of the sentences that's completely new, 'The only bit of colour was the Chinese restaurant where we queued for our sweet and sour Friday nights'. Now that was Terence applying his own knowledge of suburban small town Australia in the 1970s which, of course, I don't have and which didn't emerge in the oral history... I remember people would laugh appreciatively at that. So that sort of stuff people liked.

TERENCE: It's not a realistic drama in any sense. It has a poetic and imaginative sense to it. The original production was a beautiful, beautiful-looking show... and its look was very much a part of it as well. Although the material is so strong you could do it in a bare room with five chairs and it would still work. Generally speaking *Minefields* was really well received and critically really well received but there were some people – and it was in a minority but they were loud – who said, 'It's not theatre because it's just talking heads'. And they completely missed the point as if we'd failed in making a play... It was meant to be this shared experience with an audience where the characters spoke quite literally to the audience of their journey and they're surrounded by theatrical and atmospheric trappings. [I worry about] all those clichés that people say like, 'Drama needs to show not tell', and all those sort of laws about what theatre's supposed to be.

SIOBHAN: The feedback from audiences... they love it. They really identify with the women... Now I think a lot of the reality comes from the fact that they are very real experiences. So when [the nurse] gets the POW and she's reflecting on her mixed feelings about having treated a woman who she knows was responsible for some act that may have killed a child and then she talks about another bloke and she says, 'I had to do the amputation because the surgeon was so hung-over'. That was amazing. And then she says, 'We heard later he was taken away and hanged, I was really pissed off because I trimmed it off really nicely'. That sort of black humour has got to be real.

ROSLYN: You couldn't write that.

SIOBHAN: They were the sort of things that Terence honed in on very skillfully, I think. It's the little minutiæ and I think you need that. When you have the grand stuff [sets, songs, soundtracks, etc.], you need to counter-balance them and weight them in this personal detail that gives it that real sense of familiarity and recognition. That's where [the play] is a good marriage.

Debra Byrne, Tracy Bartram, Tracy Mann, Wendy Stapleton and Robyn Arthur in 2004 Playbox Theatre production of *Minefields and Miniskirts*. (Photo: Lisa Tomasetti)

Errata

On page 57 in Exercise 3: Adaptation and authorship, Siobhan McHugh is speaking about the book, rather than the play, when she claims authorship. McHugh and O'Connell agree that McHugh is the author of the book, and O'Connell is the author of the play, and that they are two separate creative works. Please make the following substitute for the first two paragraphs:

The play *Minefields and Miniskirts* is a successful adaptation, which worked well in the eyes of both oral historian Siobhan McHugh and playwright Terence O'Connell. Here's what they say about authorship of the two different creative works, the book and the play:

> **SIOBHAN:** I feel I'm the author [of the book]. There's multiple inputs. *Minefields and Miniskirts* contains the stories of fifty people. It would be nothing without those fifty stories. But those stories on their own... neither would they have made a book. So what was required was actually, somebody to thread them all together into a kind of tapestry.

On page 86, the third sentence under Step 4 Editing should read 'The interviewer's (rather than interviewee's) voice should be removed wherever possible.'

B) **CLASS DISCUSSION TOPICS AND EXERCISES**

Exercise 1: The Vietnam War

Question family members who were born before 1955 about the Vietnam War.

- Ask them about conscription, and what they thought of the justification of the war. Were they involved themselves?
- Go on to ask whether they were aware of the involvement of Australian women directly in the war, or have recollections of how women in Australia were affected.

Exercise 2: What's in a title?

I like 'minefields' because it was both the literal minefield and the kind of emotional minefields that go into what war presents. So once I got the notion of minefields I looked around and 'miniskirts' not only had the female element, it had the sixties, it had the era, so it was great.

Siobhan McHugh

- As you explore the play, identify specific elements which convey the theme of 'the sixties'. Develop your own stage design for a performance to emphasise this theme.
- Compare the way the play conveys Australian history and culture with what you would encounter in a textbook. Discuss.

Exercise 3: Adaptation and authorship

Minefields and Miniskirts is a successful adaptation, which worked well in the eyes of both oral historian Siobhan McHugh and playwright Terence O'Connell. But there's one thing that perhaps they don't quite agree about. When asked who is the 'author' of play, here's what they said:[75]

SIOBHAN: I feel I'm the author. There's multiple inputs. Like *Minefields and Miniskirts*, the book contains the stories of fifty people. It would be nothing without those fifty stories. But those stories on their own... neither would they have made a book. So what was required was actually, somebody to thread them all together into a kind of tapestry.

TERENCE: I consider myself to be the author of the play. Obviously in everything that's written about it, it says 'adapted from Siobhan's book'. But as well, the dialogue and – I don't know, I've never really looked at this but I imagine – maybe ten percent, maybe fifteen percent of the dialogue is actually from me anyway. But it's obviously adapted from Siobhan's book and consequently from the women's memories and interviews. I suppose the authorship of [the play] is about the look of it and the sound of it. In that sense, someone has to be called the author so I guess I do.

Discuss what may at first seem to be different perspectives above. (See also Chapter 15: Ethics, Ownership, Authorship.)
- How important is it to agree on authorship?
- What is your view about the authorship of *Minefields and Miniskirts*?

C) **RESOURCES FOR FURTHER STUDY**

Selected material about the Vietnam War

There is an extensive literature on the Vietnam War. All recent histories of the twentieth century include material. What follows is a small selection, and you are encouraged to make your own broader historical study.

Australian Government, Australia and the Vietnam War. http://vietnam-war.commemoration.gov.au

Murphy, John. *Harvest of Fear*: A History of Australia's Vietnam War, Sydney: Allen and Unwin 1993.

For information about the 1987 Welcome Home March, go to http://vietnam-war.commemoration.gov.au/commemoration

An 'unofficial' veterans' perspective is at www.diggerhistory.info/pages-conflicts-periods/vietnam/welcome-home.htm

Vietnam Veterans Association www.vvaa.org.au/

Veterans Wives group http://home.vicnet.net.au/~vietnet/Resources.html

Lucas, Adam (ed.). *Viet Nam Voices: Australians and the Vietnam War*, Sydney: Casula Powerhouse Arts Centre 2000

'In Place of War'

Minefields and Miniskirts is one of many recent creative works about aspects of war. For access to other examples, you might like to visit the website of the 'In Place of War' program, based in Manchester. This program brings together playwrights and other creative artists from more than 40 countries who are devising works related to all facets of war, from battlefields to home fronts, from parliaments to refugee camps, from child soldier training grounds to detention centres. Access it at www.inplaceofwar.net

8.

Parramatta Girls:

Verbatim Theatre about the Forgotten Australians

ROSLYN OADES

A) **THE PLAY IN CONTEXT**

Parramatta Girls (2007) traces the legacy of eight Australian women who were cruelly institutionalised in a state home for 'uncontrollable' girls. As teenagers at the notorious Girls Training School in Parramatta, they suffered at the hands of abusive carers and were subjected to intrusive physical examinations, intense manual workloads, excessive punishments and appalling conditions. We now refer to these neglected girls, and the 500,000 Australian children like them who were placed in orphanages or reform homes between 1930 and 1970, as the 'Forgotten Australians'. Inspired by a TV journalist's story on an actual Parramatta Girls reunion, Alana Valentine went on to spend four years researching this project. She was particularly motivated by the extent to which the real women's stories 'hadn't been believed'. Her creative process was driven by a desire to 'articulate [the] unspoken things' these women lived with.

> I was really keen to hang out around a whole lot of older women, you know? Who had been through a lot – that was just really missing in my life and they'd all had a really really tough time and yet they were enormously enormously funny. That was again something I was really familiar with as a kind of way of being. And so I didn't need to capture their exact voice, I had to capture the spirit, the soul, the way of being in the world that those women were and that's why I chose a sort of massaged verbatim form. So I didn't just want it to be me writing these women, I wanted it to be based on what they said and how they felt and this very real chapter of Australian history which is appalling. But in terms of why choose a verbatim play, why not just write a play about a whole lot of women in a home and what they experienced? It was because I wanted that personal contact, you know, with those women.
>
> *Alana Valentine, playwright,* **Parramatta Girls**

Development

Parramatta Girls is Valentine's second verbatim play. On this project she explores a form she terms 'massaged verbatim', as opposed to the 'pure verbatim' style employed on her previous work, *Run Rabbit Run* (2004), in which interviewees' stories are faithfully transcribed and presented as they were told by real people. In *Parramatta Girls*, Valentine shapes her collected interviews around an invented narrative structure. She describes this framework as very simple: a group of ex-Parramatta Girls 'come to the reunion, they look around, they leave'. This loose character journey provides Valentine with a structure from which to explore the dramatic potential of memories and personalities colliding as we trace each woman's personal struggle to both look back and move forward with their lives.

> I just started going to a lot of the Parramatta Girls' events. Then there was a reunion actually out at the Home in November, which I went to, talked to a whole lot of women there, gave out flyers about the project... and just started getting to know them. There were two things, first I couldn't believe this had happened, that this excruciating treatment of children in Australia – which has had a long history in Australia, you know – had been happening as recently as 1974. I just thought that it was unconscionable. So I wanted to tell their story but I also just thought it was this amazing camaraderie between the Indigenous and non-Indigenous women.
>
> *Alana Valentine*

Valentine's starting point was to personally interview as many of the original Parramatta Girls as she could track down. Drawing on the authentic vernacular and anecdotes of over thirty-five women, Valentine then 'collapsed' her source material into eight distinct characters. During her interview process she found herself focusing on the stories of a core group of women, who later became the basis for her characters. The real names of these core interviewees appear as character names in the play as a way of 'honouring' their profound contribution – despite representing an amalgamation of stories. The obvious exception is the character of Maree, who in the world of the play, exists only in the past. Although based on the life of a real girl who died in the home (as relayed to Valentine by fellow inmates), the character of Maree is an invention.

> The first reading I had at Belvoir Street was literally just their testimony, cut up and arranged a bit like pure verbatim in *Run Rabbit Run*. And it was only as I started to interview more and more women and started to see patterns in what they told me and in the way they coped that I realised that I could start to collapse the stories together and it didn't need to be the pure

verbatim. But the first reading needed to be pure verbatim for them to go, 'OK this is my voice'. There was an invited audience to the reading – they heard it. So, I guess that's another way verbatim is different from, you know, just writing a normal play in which the public readings are often for the writer to see where the holes are. This was really for the community to build trust and allow me to then start collapsing [characters]. It was like gaining their trust and helping them to understand that they were going to be heard and now they didn't actually, necessarily have to be heard exactly.

Alana Valentine

Valentine's reasoning behind her 'massaged verbatim' approach on *Parramatta Girls* relates to her sense of ethical responsibility and the desire to tell a shared story as opposed to focusing on the potentially voyeuristic horror of individual trauma. Her narrative choice to alternate between past and present action shifts the work away from being read solely as documentary theatre and into a more traditionally lyrical play style. Yet, despite the author's obvious creative input, to an Australian audience the inclusion of local place names, recent historical facts, unflinchingly gruesome details and the distinctly familiar mannerisms of verbatim speech (peppered with a good deal of gallows humour too odd to invent), endows the text with a weighty sense of authenticity.

The creative development of the project was a long-term process and involved three public showings of work-in-progress prior to the play's first season. The community participants who had contributed their stories were invited to each public showing and asked to contribute their feedback, alongside Company B's creative team.

The script underwent several very different incarnations before the final version was realised. The first draft presented was in a 'pure verbatim' form, which involved the actors faithfully retelling the women's stories as a direct address to the audience. Valentine reflects that her first audience 'were horrified that this had happened in Australia, to women who were still alive'. In the second draft presented (at Company B's 2004 Winter Play Reading Series), Valentine included stories from some of the women's children and the guards from the institution as a means of exploring the ongoing legacy of the women's experience.

> I started to write characters which were the guards. So I started writing all these people around the women and we had another public reading. And that was starting to find these narratives, trying to take the disparate interviews and put the narratives together. And afterwards, Neil Armfield said to me, 'I can see what you're trying to do and it's really interesting but, you

know, honestly we're not interested in anything other than the women. We really just want to hear the women. We know that their children are important and, yes, it's kind of interesting the legacy, but really we just want to hear from the women'. So I went away and wrote another draft where I started to construe relationships between the women.

Alana Valentine

Taking advice from director Neil Armfield onboard, Valentine's third draft presentation (at Company B's 2005 Winter Play Reading Series) just followed the stories of the women. This draft focused on building up relationships between the characters and creating fictional scenes. As well as providing a means of building the play, these public showings also allowed Valentine the opportunity to build trust with the community participants. It was important to her that the women were involved in this process and fully aware and accepting of the collapsed stories device she employed. Valentine says of the verbatim playwright, 'You're both a participant and an observer. You have to be aware that you are participating in their lives and their history'.

Production and reception

Parramatta Girls premiered at the Belvoir Street Theatre, Sydney, under the direction of Wesley Enoch in March 2007. It received excellent press reviews. Bryce Hallet for the *Sydney Morning Herald* wrote: '*Parramatta Girls* is desperately sad, honest, humorous and uplifting. It is a triumph for Valentine and company. On opening night, when former inmates joined the actors on stage for the curtain call, there were tears, smiles and slightly embarrassed bows; an extraordinary moment of life and art blurring and uniting as one'. Much of the rhetoric surrounding this first production of *Parramatta Girls*, which predates the national apology to Forgotten Australians in 2009, makes use of two words: honest and healing. Valentine reiterated this sentiment, relaying several moving accounts from participants, their families and the broader community of Forgotten Australians who expressed a profound appreciation at being heard and believed. 'They loved being believed, that was the most important thing... On the opening night [one of the participants] came up to me and said, "You've given me back the twelve year old girl that was taken from me".'

> **ROSLYN:** What do you think you'd identify as the key creative challenge of making *Parramatta Girls*?
> **ALANA:** I think just not making it a litany of miserable suffering. Distilling with integrity the spirit of those women, which is, like I say, very very funny but also very painful. Perversely, also not lightening it too much; not making it too palatable; not... looking away from the horror and the utter shattering of lives.

And that's why I included a character who died, because there were plenty of people who didn't make it through... not just in the homes but later, especially, who took their own lives. And, you know, honouring the horror of that without sort of merely making it this kind of catalogue of horrors. Which I think would have actually not been as theatrically effective. You know because audiences become very indifferent after a while. And I was really keen not to play on that in the piece. There was a lot of suggestion of violence. You know, I wasn't flinching, I wasn't looking away from the horror but I just don't think there's any reason to glorify it. And I also think it makes it about the perpetrator. Then you make a play about the perpetrators and their victims. And these women were so far from victims. You know, I just wanted to show the damage and the effect of what had happened. So the creative challenge for this play really was to not just make it a litany of horrors that had happened in the past. To show what the effect was on them and their survival and their community now... I hope that people would find a way to connect about that experience. I would hope that people would leave with a strong sense of determination for this never to happen again. You know, people who are in policy-making positions or politicians or social workers. I would hope that parents would leave cherishing the relationships that they have with their children. That mothers who give themselves a hard time about not doing enough for their children might go easy on themselves and think, 'You know what, I'm actually doing OK'. You know, so many different things. I suppose I really would like people to see these women as survivors and see how tough and courageous it is.

B) *CLASS DISCUSSION, TOPICS AND EXERCISES*

Authenticity and performance

Parramatta Girls is one of the few verbatim plays that does not rely on actors delivering direct address (or testimony) to the audience, though it certainly relies on characters telling stories to each other. Also, unlike *The Laramie Project*, all evidence of the writer's interview process has been omitted from the performance script.

- Does Valentine's 'massaged verbatim' approach cause us to sense the authenticity in the play? How does it do this?
- Compare and contrast the different modes of delivering 'truth' in *The Laramie Project* and *Parramatta Girls*.

- See also Chapter 12: Memory, Truth and Authenticity for further exercises.

Dramatic shape

Alana Valentine describes her narrative framework for *Parramatta Girls* as a simple journey: a group of old girls attend a reunion, look around and then go home.

- What other possible storytelling structure could she have investigated to support her source material? For example, consider the material shaped around a court case into Maree's death or set in the audience of Prime Minister Kevin Rudd's national apology to The Forgotten Australians in 2009.
- Discuss the relationship between memory and dramatic structure in *Parramatta Girls*.

Staging

Bryce Hallett in his review for the *Sydney Morning Herald* describes the set for the Company B production of *Parramatta Girls* as follows: 'Ralph Myers' stripped-to-the-bone set, with its stacks of metal chairs, starkly symbolises the ruin and discarding of souls'. From the photos in the playtext, we can see that a predominately naturalistic approach was taken in regard to this production's use of staging and props. There are images depicting copper laundry basins, a single bed, sheets, brooms, rubber gloves, stacks of metal school chairs and a piano in the corner. The actors also appear to wear uniform white aprons over their 'adult clothes' in various scenes to indicate a return to the past.

- Discuss alternative approaches to the staging of this work.
- In what ways could the transitions between past and present be demonstrated in performance?

Social context and community

Parramatta Girls was written two years before Prime Minister Kevin Rudd's national apology to the Forgotten Australians.

- Listen to Kevin Rudd's apology, made on 16 November 2009, and discuss what impact you think this event would have had on the women in the play.
- How can a play like *Parramatta Girls* have a direct impact on government policy?
- See also Chapter 14: Verbatim Theatre and Community.

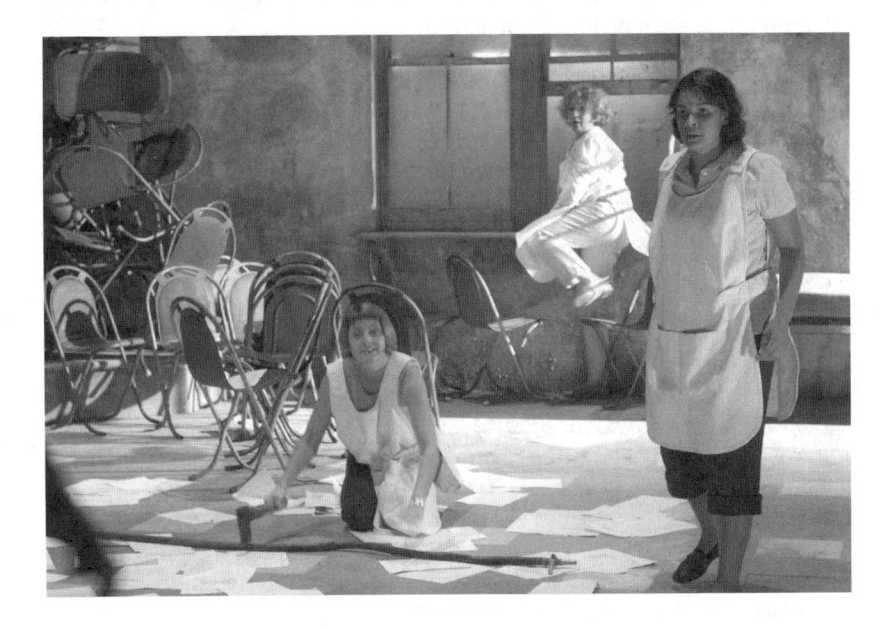

Jeanette Cronin, Annie Byron and Lisa Flanagan in the 2007 Company B production of *Parramatta Girls*. (Photo: Heidrun Löhr)

Audience engagement

On the opening night of *Parramatta Girls* at Belvoir Street Theatre, the community participants were invited to join the actors on stage and share in the audience's applause. This was a powerful indicator of the project's profound community engagement.

- If you were to stage your own production of *Parramatta Girls*, would you make links with the people Valentine interviewed and involve them in the production?
- In what other ways could this sense of genuine engagement with living Australian history be achieved?
- Do you think verbatim plays have a relevance outside the community upon which they are based? How well do they travel? How can one community send a 'message' to another?

C) RESOURCES FOR FURTHER STUDY

The real Parramatta Girls Home www.parragirls.org.au/

Hogson, Rosalie. 'Home Girls Have Their Say' Introduction to the Playscript. *Parramatta Girls*. Sydney: Currency Press 2007.

Care Leavers Australia Network (CLAN), A network for people who grew up in Australian orphanages, Children's Homes and in foster care. www.clan.org.au

Prime Minister Kevin Rudd's Apology to the Forgotten Australians: www.abc.net.au/news/video/2009/11/16/2743730.htm

ABC coverage of the Forgotten Australians speech, with valuable links to other material:
www.abc.net.au/news/stories2009/11/16/2743742.htm

Bryce Hallett's *Sydney Morning Herald* Review (23rd March 2007) www.smh.com.au/news/arts-reviews/parramatta-girls/2007/03/23/1174597831915.html

Captivated by Reality, Alana Valentine delivers the 2009 Alex Buzo Memorial Lecture: www.usyd.edu.au/sydney_ideas/lectures/2009/captivated_reality.shtml

Anderson, Michael and Linden Wilkinson. 'A Resurgence of Verbatim Theatre: Authenticity, Empathy and Transformation' *Australasian Drama Studies* 50 (2007): 153–169.

9.

Run Rabbit Run:

Voices from the Heartland of Rugby League

Paul Dwyer

A) **THE PLAY IN CONTEXT**

In November 2000, the 'Red and Green Army' invaded the Sydney central business district: a crowd of 80,000 people hitting the streets in protest against a Federal Court decision which had ruled that News Limited – a major shareholder of the privatised National Rugby League (also the Australian subsidiary of News Corp, one of the world's most powerful corporations) – could kick the under-performing South Sydney 'Rabbitohs' out of the NRL competition. Two years later, after further legal action (costing millions of dollars, much of it coming from grassroots fundraising, plus a few high-profile patrons), the Rabbitohs supporters managed to get their team reinstated. Some people – a lot of people – love their footy.

The playwright, Alana Valentine, is one. She describes herself as someone 'brought up in a working-class, football-attending family... a South's supporter living in the St George area'. Later, during her university days, the words 'football' and 'culture' were rarely heard in the same sentence: 'Everyone around me was talking about film theory, so the fact that you knew what the five-eighth did was irrelevant'.[76] Living in Redfern at the time of the Rabbitohs expulsion from the NRL, she recognised the palpable energy of a community finding its voice: a diverse, unstable community, to be sure, but nevertheless a groundswell of people for whom footy is indeed part of a way of life, as much a part of one's culture as religion, ethnicity or the bonds of family.

Valentine successfully pitched the idea of a verbatim play, using the struggle over Souths as a window onto the concerns of this community, to Company B whose home, the Belvoir St Theatre, is also barely a stone's throw from the South Sydney Leagues Club and the team's historic Redfern Oval base. Valentine was commissioned to conduct some preliminary interviews ('to give us a taste of the voices out there', as Chris Mead, Belvoir's Literary Manager at the time, put it) and *Run Rabbit Run* was underway: an exceptional project in which one of Australia's most prestigious theatre companies would make a show in dialogue with the community living on its doorstep, many of them the kind of 'battlers' who would rarely, if ever, have contemplated attending the theatre.[77]

Project history

Alana Valentine has described *Run Rabbit Run* as a 'pure verbatim' play: it is composed entirely of excerpts from the transcripts of interviews conducted by Valentine or else direct quotes from material in the public domain (press coverage of the issue, a News Corporation annual report, etc.). Importantly, she stresses that there was a strong dramatic purpose, as well as an ideological commitment, behind this choice of approach. It was very much a reaction to what she regards as the usually stereotypical portrayals of working-class people in mainstream theatre:

> I just thought, 'They're not like that at all, some of them are really racist but there are philosophers, they're not simple, inarticulate, you know, they're actually incredibly lucid'... I wanted to show that football fans were not these stupid, inarticulate, sports-crazy people, but were actually people of extraordinary values, kindness, community, you know, strength and purpose. And so, I felt like if I wrote those characters the way I knew them, people wouldn't believe them and so verbatim gave me this wonderful cover. An irrefutable way of representing a class of people that I knew and because I was having them speak in their own words couldn't be faulted.
>
> *Alana Valentine, playwright,* **Run Rabbit Run**

In many ways, this is where the most interesting textural qualities of the script come from. The verbatim approach reproduces all the false starts, slips and stumbling of actual conversation – Valentine's interviewees were obviously having to think on their feet – but the total effect does not portray them as inarticulate. Rather, we get a sense that language itself is almost inadequate to the task of explaining why people feel so strongly about certain things. The footy fans' moments of 'lucidity and philosophical sophistication' tend to come with the force of a hammer, breaking through the niceties of polite conversation or the intricate 'legalese' and corporate 'Newspeak' of their adversaries.

Consider, for example, the following speech of Mark Courtney, an ordinary (if somewhat obsessive) Souths fan who functions, in some ways, as a kind of 'Everyman' character in the play. He breaks through to a brief, blunt, powerful and expletive statement about this story's wider political significance. As if embarrassed that this might be taken as too much grandstanding, he then quickly plays down his credentials as a would-be political activist (although it's not too hard to imagine Mark taking to the streets again for something like the trade union campaign, 'Your Rights at Work'):

> **MARK:** I've want—I can't wait to tell my grandkids about—you know. What we did. Because there aren't that many great achievements in

people's lives. You know, so I reckon people have none sometimes. All right, you can take our bloody community bank branch, and you can take this and you can take that, and you nationalise this and you can stuff that up, but you can't take this... There's the line and it's drawn now and it's about fucking time that someone drew the line, but it's drawn, you know, and I think—it will certainly give me a belief—a core belief that things can be achieved, but it—you know, I mean, I said beforehand and, and I would—I would say it now, that I don't have the time to do as much as I would like... ah, and I don't, but somehow with this it was so important to the cause, so much, that I made the time, you know, and did it. But also, I mean, there was no football, so, you know, I had the time.

Another feature of the script is the way in which reflections on potentially very sensitive personal experiences are slipped in, almost as an afterthought, in the interviewee's conversations about Souths. Though fleeting, these remind us that, in many respects, the play is not about football. It's about the surprising moments of intimacy between neighbours (and sometimes strangers) that a feeling for football facilitates, which then becomes a resource in times of personal/community crisis. Eileen McLaughlin's speeches in Act II, sc.3, where she mentions in passing some extraordinarily tragic family event, are a good example. So too is Nick Pappas' account, towards the very end of the play, of his father's funeral. Again, Valentine describes this as one of the great attractions of verbatim play-making: 'Sometimes it's easier to sit at your desk and make it up and yet, at the same time, there is nothing like the rewards of real people. Because they are so reliably surprising. They just say and do and feel and think so many contradictory, wonderful things'.

The idea that *Run Rabbit Run* is 'pure verbatim' does not of course mean that the writer's role is any less interventionist, when it comes to creating the dramatic shape of a play, than it would be for a fictional work. Right from the beginning of the project, Valentine was making choices and a lot can be learnt from the way she structured her research and interviewing process. Her first interview subject was Norm Lipson, the former Media Manager at Souths: Valentine knew that he was used to dealing with writers and journalists, and also that he would have a lot of contacts. From there she followed what is often called a 'snowballing' technique – asking each new interview subject who else would be worth talking to. Once she had a sense of the scope of the story and some dominant opinions among the community, she started actively looking for opposing views and dissenting voices (from within the Souths community but also from other 'players' in the struggle, including News Limited executives).

She also made sure to include some group interviews as a way of ensuring that there could be some dialogue scenes to break up the 'stand and deliver' monologues which directly address the audience. It is worth noting that Valentine's suggestion in the script as to where an interval could be taken in performance means the second half opens with the often hilarious dialogue between Marcia Seebacher and her mother, Barbara Selby, about their zealous voluntary contribution to the Club's merchandising and fundraising efforts. This shifts the action of the play into a more intimate, private world (in the Belvoir St production, it stood out as the only time when two characters were alone on stage) and helps to set up later dialogue scenes like the Courtney family's group interview (performed on a picnic rug in the original production).

> There's always a dynamic within the group that is interesting to observe and dramatic when you put it on stage. I mean if you'd heard that interview with Marcia and Barbara, it wasn't actually particularly funny. It's when it's performed later as a duologue that it becomes side-splitting. And on the opening night, Marcia and Barbara, I saw them in the audience, they were just like, they were crying they were laughing so much. But at the time they weren't like that. You know, it's seeing themselves on stage and realising what a kind of double act they were in real life. Sometimes the theatrical act can heighten what happens.
>
> *Alana Valentine*

Valentine is quite candid about the fact that there came a time, late in the writing process, when she needed to find new interviewees, or to interview someone a second time, in the hope that they would utter something fairly specific in order for her to plug a perceived gap in her play's structure. This was certainly the case with Peter Macourt, whose interview, along with parts of John Hartigan's, yielded some of the most sympathetic quotes to come from a News Limited perspective. Here and elsewhere, we can see that Valentine's intention was not simply to create a 'David vs Goliath' story in which the corporate executives come across as evil stooges.

> You want the complexities... You have to think that that corporation were not just being utterly scurrilous; even if they were, it's not interesting dramatically. I needed that it was this clash between the demands of the corporatisation of sport and the attractions of tradition, the nostalgia of tradition. And I needed to lay – not blame – but ask questions about the sort of intransigent clinging to tradition and whether that was always the best option. So I needed to sort of show the fatal flaw. People always describe that in a Shakespearian character, 'What is their fatal flaw?' Well to actually look at, if *Run Rabbit Run* is about the community not about any one person; what is the fatal flaw within that community that made it hard for them to make that transition?
>
> *Alana Valentine*

Julie Hamilton and Jody Kennedy in the 2004 Company B production of *Run Rabbit Run*. (Photo: Heidrun Löhr)

Two final points about Valentine's interviewing and writing process are, firstly, that she offers this wonderful piece of advice for anyone else attempting to create a 'pure verbatim' play: 'I suppose when I'm interviewing I'm trying to get somebody to have some sort of change happen within them. Or, when they tell a story to have some sort of transformation so that there is an internal drama'. Secondly, the task of selecting, editing and refining transcript material, through successive drafts of the script, involved not only checking back with interviewees to see that they were happy with how the material was being used but also close collaboration with the director, actors and other Company B staff. So much so that a read-through of the draft script, on the first day of rehearsals, ran for about seven hours. As Valentine explains it, she knew that there would have to be enormous amounts of material cut from this draft but she also needed her collaborators to take part in the culling process so that the finished play would retain a sense of the larger world, of which the play is merely a thin slice.

> *Run Rabbit Run* has a found structure as well. It starts with [the team] being kicked out. It regresses a little bit to what set that up and it goes back to the moment where they start to fight. So I had the found structure I would call it: the first injunction which they lost; the trial, which they lost; the appeal which they won. And I personally think that some of the best verbatim plays are plays that have those sort of series of public events cladding the rest of the work. A lot of verbatim work that doesn't work for me is when it's about a subject. No play is about a subject, it's always about human nature and what the drama reveals of human nature.
>
> *Alana Valentine*

Production history

As described above, *Run Rabbit Run* was a highly unusual cross between a grassroots, community-based performance project and a mainstage production in one of the country's most famous venues. The first production (the only professional production at the time of publication) premiered at the Belvoir St on 7 January 2004.[78] The theatre's location, not only geographically but also in terms of what we might call 'social space', certainly contributed to the play's significance for the large number of audience members who came from the South Sydney area. When the actor playing Jimmy Lahood, for example, stood centre stage and started pointing out his character's local roots ('I was born in Redfern, my dad went to school at Cleveland St High...'), many audience members knew precisely the direction in which these places lay.

However, Company B, the resident company of Belvoir St, also had a track-record in staging verbatim plays which, in many ways, prepared the ground for this particular approach to engaging the community on its doorstep. In 1993, the company's then Artistic Director, Neil Armfield, directed *Aftershocks* by Paul Brown and the Workers Cultural Action Committee, and in 2001 Kate Gaul was a guest director for Company B's Australian premiere production of *The Laramie Project*. At Armfield's suggestion, Kate Gaul was also appointed to direct *Run Rabbit Run* and, not surprisingly, she chose to work with some of the same artists: Brian Thomson, a world-renowned designer who had created the sets for both *Aftershocks* and *The Laramie Project*, plus the actors Eliza Logan and Josef Ber.

ROSLYN: Maybe we should start by having you describing your design.

BRIAN: Well it was essentially, again, it was the corner of Belvoir Street Theatre. The stage was covered in real grass.

ROSLYN: Real grass? You had to water?

BRIAN: Yes, with white lights on it.

ROSLYN: Did it smell like...?

BRIAN: Yeah, it had this fantastic smell, it was wonderful like that. And basically, the whole walls were covered in framed photographs of teams, jumpers, memorabilia and stuff. So that every square inch of Belvoir Street wall... stage walls and going right into the audience was completely covered with stuff.

ROSLYN: So all the way to the foyer?

BRIAN: All the way around. It was...

ROSLYN: Where did they come from?

BRIAN: Well these came from various collectors and a lot of it came from the Club. They had all this stuff in a basement that had all been water damaged. In a lot of cases we had to reframe a lot of stuff. Or we had to kind of almost recreate it. It was just too crappy. For then suddenly we'd hear, 'Oh, someone's got a garage full of stuff in wherever'. And we would borrow that. And we had a massive, literally the whole stage, when we were getting the stage in, was completely covered in all these things. We wondered if they'd all go, and what would have prominence. And there were a couple of long red and green benches.

ROSLYN: Like a team might sit on?

BRIAN: Like a team might have sat on, yes. In the olden... not like they do now.

ROSLYN: A bit nostalgic.

BRIAN: It was very much to suggest the family Club and an extension of a suburb, of a community, in that kind of tribal way.

Thomson's work on *Run Rabbit Run* was deceptively simple but reflects a deep understanding not only of the venue's characteristics and of verbatim as a genre but also of the play's social function with respect to the local community. Belvoir St Theatre has a large, very open, roughly diamond-shaped stage that juts out from a corner of the room into the auditorium, with audience on three sides in raked seating benches. It is a space that fits well with the convention of direct address to the audience and which also favours elements such as a floor covering or fairly flat design features on the back walls rather than an elaborate set design cluttering up the main playing areas. Such constraints often work as a productive stimulus. Thomson's design, using real grass and abundant 'found' memorabilia, meant that audience members who came from the local area and were not regular Belvoir St patrons walked into a space with which they could feel an immediate connection. This feeling of being in your own community permeated each performance.

> There was a young man who used to bring his life-sized rabbit and book a seat for the rabbit. And he came two or three times. I mean South's supporters would bring their kids and they would talk to the actors. They would often boo and the actors would have to yell back, 'Oh, give us a chance!' You know, which was really great. There was almost always some South's supporters in the audience. I think the Belvoir patrons... I mean quite a lot of, I've got to say, Belvoir patrons are mature-aged women who wouldn't normally go a see a play about football. I know that Neil [Armfield] told me a couple of stories about marching people over to the box office and saying, 'You've got to see this play'. Because they were like, 'Oh, who cares?' I mean I had women come up to me, clutching my arm, crying, saying, 'I hate football but I loved your play'[fake sobbing]. You know, because the play wasn't about football but to them, a play *Run Rabbit Run*, with red and green was going to be about that... At interval, the actors would go off stage and the audience would walk straight onto the stage. I mean, no problems with that, they'd walk up and have a look at all the memorabilia that was on the back of the stage and all around. So they hung around inside.
>
> *Alana Valentine*

B) **CLASS DISCUSSION TOPICS AND EXERCISES**

Social context and community

Eliza Logan, who has acted in several verbatim plays including *The Laramie Project*, has this to say about her own experience of *Run Rabbit Run*:

And when we came to doing *Run Rabbit Run* it was like, 'Oh yeah, but you know, it's just a footy team – is it really that important?' But then you read the words, you go, 'Oh, OK'. And you keep immersing yourself into that world and meeting some of the people and remembering like Granny like stuff like that who were ferocious footy fans and you go, 'Oh no – this is life blood as well'. It just seems possibly odd if you're not a sports fan. But it's not just a sport, it's actually a way of life, it is the heart of their community. And so, in that respect, it was actually quite a great learning for me.

Eliza Logan

- How easily can you immerse yourself in the stories of someone else's community?
- As a creative artist staging the play, how would you approach the task of engaging 'outsiders' (even someone who hates sport!) in *Run Rabbit Run*?
- Do you think there is a sense in which *Run Rabbit Run* helped develop the community's capacity to undertake political protest? Discuss.
- See Chapter 14: Verbatim Theatre and Community for more exercises.

Dramatic shape

Above, in this chapter, there is a quote from Alana Valentine about the simple 'found structure' in *Run Rabbit Run*. She is suggesting how real events create a 'cladding' for verbatim plays, which then must explore human nature within that structure.

- How has she edited transcript material to give individual characters a journey?
- What are some of these journeys? Try to map out how they weave through the overall structure.
- Do you think these character journeys achieve the exploration of human nature that Valentine is pursuing? How?

Sport moves centre stage

- You might like to make a survey of Australian plays which are about sport, or which include references to sports people. Start with David Williamson's *The Club*, or *Shane Warne: The Musical*.
- Compare Alana Valentine's verbatim approach with what other playwrights have done to bring the theme of sport to the stage. What are the advantages, or limitations, of these different approaches?

C) RESOURCES FOR FURTHER STUDY

Chris Mead, in his illuminating introduction to the *Run Rabbit Run* playscript, indicates that Company B set out quite deliberately to 'engage more fully with the community on its doorstep'. In exploring the context for *Run Rabbit Run*, you might like to investigate the forms of community theatre prevalent in Australia. To this end, visit the website of the Australia Council for the Arts for information about community cultural development, or go direct to the site of Community Cultural Development Australia www.ccd.net/

It's not hard to find press coverage of the year 2000 controversy over the status of the South Sydney Club. It was covered extensively in the media, and you might head first to the Daily Telegraph archives. The debate moved all the way to the Federal Parliament, and to see what was discussed there, go to the speech in the House of Representatives by MP Anthony Albanese: http://parlinfo.aph.gov.au:80/parlInfo/genpdf/chamber/hansardr/1999-10-18/0149/hansard_frag.pdf;fileType%3Dapplication%2F.pdf

We could think of *Run Rabbit Run* as a play which makes a contribution to Australian history, in which case there are rich resources from the field of sports studies. For a wealth of items about Rugby League, including the South Sydney Club in particular, visit the national museum site: http://library.nma.gov.au/libero/docs/Libopac/bibliographies_files/rugbybib2.htm

Alex Buzo is another well-known Australian playwright who was interested in sport and history. See his lecture: Buzo, Alex. 'Sydney, Heart of Rugby League: Third Annual Tom Brock Lecture, 2001'. Also published in *More than a Game*, Syson, Ian (ed.) *Overland* 166 (2002): pp.35–41.

Part Three

Workshops for Exploring Themes and Issues

Valerie Bader, Lisa Flanagan and Leah Purcell in the 2007 Company B production of Parramatta Girls. (Heidrun Löhr)

Following are six workshops designed to stimulate thinking, discussion and verbatim theatre practice.

The first two workshops provide specific suggestions for making plays. The other four workshops lean more towards discussion of ideas and themes that will be relevant to the study of plays set for the high school curriculum.

The best approach to these workshops will be to adapt them freely to suit classroom timetables and individual styles of learning and teaching.

These six workshops will start a collection which we hope will grow on the Currency Press website, where other models and practical suggestions will be added as our own experience widens, and as teachers and other practitioners contribute what has worked for them.

10.

Making a Verbatim Play

WORKSHOP BY PAUL BROWN

This is a plan for making a piece of verbatim theatre in a learning and teaching context, exploring the challenges and issues of verbatim through discussion and debate. The plan was first used in a one-day seminar for the Drama Teachers Association of NSW. Here it is set out as three workshop sessions needing up to a full day for each session; but the work could be structured in various ways to suit available time. At the outset, participants should be told that what they learn from the process is more important than producing a finished verbatim play.

Session 1: Preparing for 'Real Life' Interviews

This first workshop session will need a number of recording devices. Allow for one between every two people.

Opening and introductions

Begin with a discussion of plays (or films) participants have seen which include 'real life' material. The facilitator might then explain verbatim as a technique within the broader scope of reality and documentary theatre. This could move to introduce the basic process: how the interviews are conducted, how they then become transcripts, and, finally, the staged performance. Build the discussion around extracts from existing verbatim plays, if possible with access to original transcripts. (See the Currency Verbatim website for transcripts from selected plays: www.currency.com.au/verbatimwebsite.aspx)

What works as verbatim theatre?

Working in groups of three, discuss ideas for a verbatim play. Bring these to the whole group. Have a discussion about what works as verbatim theatre. Possibilities on the table are likely to include current 'high level' political controversies, stories of injustice inflicted against an individual or a group, explorations of 'hidden voices' within a community, recollections about particular, often catastrophic, events. Bring the discussion to a point around the idea that the verbatim arena is populated by 'people who care about injustice'. If possible, move to consensus on a project which suits your group.

Setting up the project
Consider the issue of control over the material (see Chapter 15: Ethics, Ownership, Authorship). Try to make decisions about who will and will not be involved as interviewees and interviewers, the roles of steering groups, writers, directors and actors, and ethical issues associated with working with 'real life'. Consider practical and ethical issues associated with designing interviews. Discuss the distinction between information, opinion, reflection and anecdote, and why anecdote is the verbatim writer's best friend. Develop around five or six key questions which you think will bring out dramatic material.

First interviews
Conduct short practice interviews for your agreed project – initially these could be done amongst participants if the project relates to their experience, with people working in pairs to interview each other. Include a mock-up of what interviewers might say when asking someone to tell their story.

Next steps
Makes some decisions about the conduct and timetable of the whole project. From this, establish how and when you will conduct the main interviews, and assign tasks for completion before the second session. An example might be that each member of the group is assigned to do some general research about the topic, and to try to conduct one or two interviews with people who wish to tell their story. Ground rules for approaching interviewees need to be established. Release forms need to be available (see samples on pages 117–8), as does recording equipment. Facilitators need to be prepared to advise and possibly debrief participants as interviews proceed.

Session 2: Transcribing, Editing, Structuring
The second session explores the craft of the verbatim play-makers in some detail, while covering several of the key questions often asked about verbatim theatre. These include:
- What passes for truth in verbatim theatre?
- What are the ethical issues in bringing real people's stories onto a public stage?
- To what extent does the verbatim dramatist remain an author?
- What are the implications of the mainstreaming of verbatim?
- Is there a danger in celebrity-making?
- Is verbatim superior to journalism?

Report back
Discuss your progress with the interviews and other project development. Now that the group has a set of taped interviews, play back a selection to

get the feel of the voices. Brainstorm key ideas for shaping your own play, suggesting possible themes and story arcs.

The vernacular, voiceprint, voices, and characters

Discuss, with examples from a number of verbatim plays, the distinctions between playtext and real-life speech. Study first-hand accounts by playwrights. You will find interview transcripts at the Currency Press verbatim website.

Transcriptions

Either individually or in pairs, transcribe the group's taped interviews. Transcribing can be expected to take up to four hours for every hour of tape, so logistics will dictate whether it can proceed on the day or needs to be undertaken outside of workshop time. You will need to make a judgment about when transcribing should be accomplished before this second session takes place.

Drama and structure, construction and truth

This part of the workshop is dependent upon how familiar participants already are with storytelling and play structures. One or two verbatim plays might be used as examples, essentially to show that they follow 'rules' of drama to the same extent as any play or film. Discuss the extent to which the playwright 'constructs' a verbatim story/play, and the idea that there is greater 'truth' in a verbatim play than there is in other genres of drama. How could you best balance the tension between being 'true' to real life experience and making 'good drama'?

Structuring your own play

Working in groups of three, discuss possible ways to structure a verbatim play from the interview material. Where is the heart of this project? What is the 'climax' suggested by the material? How should the play be sculpted, based upon the material? Bring these ideas to the whole group.

Verbatim theatre: a theatre of justice

The theme of justice permeates commentary on verbatim plays, and the plays themselves. Discuss the implications of this in small groups, using commentary from creative artists who worked on the set HSC plays with selected extracts from these plays. Return to the questions at the beginning of this session – have they been addressed? Allow time for further discussion if required.

Towards a script

The second session should conclude with decision-making about how the group's play will be devised from this point. Will you have a writing team? Or a single writer/editor? How close to agreement is the group when it comes to key themes or particular story arcs? Which characters will be in the play? Do you need composite characters? How do you hope to construct dialogue out of what are commonly monologue interviews? What are the particular ethical issues in this project? Will you need to leave characters out, or edit the interview transcripts to create drama? End with serious plotting. It would be best to arrive at Session 3 armed with a working draft.

Session 3: Developing, Staging, Performing

The final session will focus on the problems associated with staging verbatim plays, and questions about the relationship between the play-makers and the audience. The role of the actor/s in verbatim theatre is clearly central to this. It would be ideal if the third session could take place after a working draft of a verbatim play has been written. If the workshop needs to be condensed, though, it is possible to conduct it focusing on the process, rather than the end result of producing a verbatim play.

Report back and reading

What is the state of play? What can we hope to achieve by the end of the day? A full performance? A revised script? A workshop reading that will be the basis of future work? Whatever stage the work is at, give it a read through, and with a sense of performance! Verbatim theatre, more than some other forms, works remarkably well as 'reader's theatre'.

The storyteller's space

Without exception, accounts of verbatim theatre practice give emphasis to the storyteller role each actor must play, and just about every verbatim play uses direct address to the audience as the principal mode of delivery. Based on your own script reading, how does it feel to work as a 'storyteller'? After this discussion, move on to consider the physical space in which verbatim plays can/should be presented. Are there any norms? Most descriptions of verbatim productions indicate very simple settings and sparse use of props and costumes. Why do most companies decide to proceed in this minimalist way? Compare verbatim with other storytelling forms.

The actor-audience relationship in verbatim theatre

Using extracts from written plays, along with commentary from artists and, if possible, the people whose stories have been told, discuss the range of experiences reported from verbatim work. Compare the verbatim experience with the functioning of 'asides' in Shakespeare's plays; or the way 'distancing' works in a Brecht play, or the tradition of the Middle-Eastern 'Hakawati' – the storyteller poets who entertain with nothing more than a stick. Consider the proposition that audiences 'listen more intently' and in a more deliberative way when they hear the words of 'real people' delivered by actors.

Towards a performance

It's now time to finalise your own play, as far as it is possible within the workshop environment. Work in groups of three, then as a whole group to brainstorm how the play or a reading of material should be staged. Cast the play, and appoint a director(s). Rehearse, pausing to re-write if time permits. The outcome is determined by the group, the time available, and the material on hand.

Conclusion

Where will the group and the project go from here?

11.
Creating a Headphone-Verbatim Performance
WORKSHOP BY ROSLYN OADES

The following is a guide to creating a series of short headphone-verbatim performances in a classroom environment over several sessions. It is envisaged that the class will select a project theme and that students will then work independently or in small groups to record, edit and perform an audio-script.

Background

Headphone-verbatim is a paperless form of verbatim theatre featuring the faithful reproduction of speech patterns. This technique operates on the principle there is as much information embedded in *how* someone speaks, as there is in *what* they are saying.

As the name suggests, headphone-verbatim requires actors to wear headphones throughout the performance, via which they are fed a carefully edited audio-script constructed from recorded interviews. The actors recite along to this audio-script with absolute precision (like a musician following a score), recreating the exact speech patterns of the original interviewees – including every cough, stumble and pause. Rather than interpret the character, as one would with a traditional script, the role of the headphone-verbatim performer is to reproduce exactly what they hear as accurately as possible. The result is a slightly surreal form of documentary theatre that evokes the essence of the source interview with fidelity and prevents the possibility of parody – even if the performer is of a different gender, age or cultural background to the original speaker.

The headphone-verbatim form was introduced by British director, Mark Wing-Davey, in his Drama Without Paper Workshop (2001) at the London Actors Centre. This workshop had a significant impact on several of the performance-makers in attendance, including Alecky Blythe, who went on to form the United Kingdom-based company Recorded Delivery and Australian director Roslyn Oades, who has created several headphone-verbatim performances with Urban Theatre Projects (UTP) in Sydney. In the case of Oades' work, she has used the headphone-verbatim form to pursue an interest in recontextualising rarely heard or misrepresented Australian voices into positions of authority. By preserving the voiceprint and mismatching the voice with a speaker of a different gender, age or racial background, she offers her audiences the opportunity to hear community-based stories from an alternative perspective.

Examples

For samples of headphone-verbatim performances which will assist this workshop, visit:

- *Stories of Love & Hate* by Roslyn Oades (Urban Theatre Projects, 2008) www.urbantheatre.com.au/storiesofloveandhate.html
- *Fast Cars & Tractor Engines* by Roslyn Oades (UTP, 2005) www.urbantheatre.com.au/carsandtractors.html
- Alecky Blythe's United Kingdom-based company Recorded Delivery www.recordeddelivery.net

The Workshop

Before getting started, some technical requirements need to be considered. To create a headphone-verbatim performance you will need access to the following audio equipment:

- Several recording/playback devices (e.g. digital recorder, dictaphone or mini-disc recorder).
- Headphones for each performer.
- Headphone-splitters. (Splitters are the equivalent of a power-board for headphones – allowing several headphone sets to be plugged into the same playback source. Splitters are inexpensive and can be picked up at most audio shops.)
- An audio-editing program on your school computer. (Digidesign Pro-tools™ is the industry standard, but most domestic audio editing programs would be adequate.)

Welcomes

An opening discussion might stress that headphone-verbatim offers performers a fascinating opportunity to explore characters outside of their experience. Actors literally adopt the actual words, breaths and speech mannerisms of another human being, with the aim of preserving the voiceprint of a recorded interview. It is also an opportunity for the theatre-maker to explore a paperless form of writing, constructing a performance script entirely via a process of sound editing.

The Facilitator should explain that the workshop will proceed in the following five steps, doing what is possible in group meetings, but with participants also doing work away from the group as required.

Step 1. Listening

Listen to several sources of 'real-life' audio samples (i.e. as opposed to media professionals or public figures). The radio is a good place to start. Examples could include interviews with members of the public, talk back, vox pops, a love-song dedications program, etc.

Without access to visual references, discuss what you hear. What information can you derive from these voices? Can you estimate the age, gender, education, cultural background and emotional state of the speaker/s? How do they feel about being interviewed? Where are they? In the case of a group interview, what is the relationship between the interviewees?

Step 2. Selecting a theme or topic

Discuss what theme you would like to cover with your play. See 'What works as verbatim theatre' in Chapter 10: Making a Verbatim Play.

Step 3. Recording exercises

Participants are given the task of interviewing a variety of people including:

- Someone who is similar to the interviewee.
- Someone who is very different from the interviewee (e.g. different age, gender, etc).
- A small group interview (e.g. family members, group of close friends, work colleagues, etc).

Interviews should last for around 30–60 minutes and address the project's theme. It is a good idea to talk to interviewee/s in general about their lives and interests before focusing on the theme. Questions which may help the subject relax and open up could be along the lines of: 'Where did you grow up?'; 'What's your earliest memory?'; and 'What is the love of your life?'. It is important that the interviewer should try not to interrupt or overlap the speaker. The aim is to record as much clean speech as possible.

At the conclusion of each interview, the workshop participants should write a detailed description of their subject/s, including their appearance, body language, distinct mannerisms/gestures/habits, how they sat and stood, what they were wearing, what they were doing, etc.

Step 4. Editing

Discuss the principles of editing audio material. The aim is to trim recordings into engaging chunks (maximum four minutes each), without losing the rhythm and quirks of the speaker/s. The interviewees' voices should be removed wherever possible. Another consideration when editing is that audiences generally find personal anecdotes more engaging than personal opinions.

Ask your students to edit and present their favourite two–four minutes of material. The material shouldn't be transcribed – this should be a purely audio exercise.

Step 5. Performing

It is important for the performers to rehearse thoroughly before a presentation. If the audio track requires more than one actor, you will need to use a headphone-splitter so the performers can all hear the same playback simultaneously.

Although it is best not to memorise lines, the performers will need to know them as well as their favourite songs. They may not know all the words, but they will have a good idea of the rhythms and be able to anticipate what is coming up.

It is also important to resist the temptation to interpret or exaggerate any of the vocal information. A good direction is: rely on your ears and body, not your mind and emotions.

The performers need to trust that all the emotional and character details are already embedded in the audio-script and their job is to simply reproduce that audio track as accurately as possible.

They can experiment with physical interpretation though. They could choose to draw from the interviewee description notes here or trial some cross-casting.

Once everyone is fully prepared, plug in, hit play and away you go.

12.
Memory, Truth and Authenticity
WORKSHOP BY ULRIKE GARDE

This workshop is a guided discussion about how memory works. Understanding this is the key to a sophisticated exploration of truth and authenticity in verbatim theatre.

1. Let's get started! Your own memories: 'I remember…'
Here is how the workshop begins.

Exercise

- Ask your class to get together in small groups of around four–five students and, as a group, think of an event that the group, class, school or neighbourhood remembers as being important. It could be something that happened at a school camp or fair, or an event which triggered strong emotions such as the threat of a fire.
- When the group has agreed on the event, turn the memories into an ad-libbed performance to be staged for the other groups in the class. Encourage the group to use a range of performance techniques to convey to the audience what has happened, why it was important at the time and how it is still important today.
- After the performance, the group should consider the feelings involved and how they were expressed. The audience could then provide you with feedback on your performances of memories.

2. Why are memories important?

To assess the importance of memory, examine the close connection between witnessing a traumatic event of the past and sharing this experience with an audience. In *Parramatta Girls*, Judi, the first character introduced, tells a story about scabs on her elbows which could be also read as a metaphor for her memories:

> **JUDI:** I still have to be careful with them. Like, they're healed, but if I knock them or something I get… bloody, I dunno what I get… I guess, I wonder if this time they won't… you know… this time they won't heal up.

Judi's concerns about her elbows are part of a personal memory, which is embedded in the larger collective memories of other girls who spent time at memory, truth and authenticity   89

the Parramatta Girls Home. The fear that scabs, and therefore memories, will break open and bleed becomes an important device for dramatic tension in this play.

Exercise

- The class should take a close look at the language used in the plays on the reading list, finding the points of the play where characters literally say 'I remember...' and variations of that.
- Choose two plays which you have studied and discuss how and when memory is mentioned. Why do you think remembering and memories play such an important role in these texts?

3. Communicating the past

Presenting collective memories on stage may also offer opportunities to present new perspectives on a shared past event. This can be done by staging the voices of people as yet unheard, silenced or disenfranchised, or by using familiar voices but adding information that sheds new light on a past event. In this context, the concept 'communicative memory' provides us with a useful tool for analysing how such a performance might have long-term effects.

Seminal research in memory studies has been undertaken by Aleida Assmann, professor of English and comparative literature, and the egyptologist Jan Assmann. One aspect of their theory is particularly important: when a group shares common memories and images of the past, this creates a feeling of 'belonging' among the group's members.[80] In other words, shared memories create group 'identities' which can be communicated in a variety of ways, such as orally, in writing, through images and in performance.

Exercise

- Which days in the calendar mark events of Australia's past that help to create a sense of shared identity?
- Which groups of the population do these events include and exclude?
- How are these days celebrated and which aspects are particularly performance-based?
- Could any of these celebrations be changed? If so, how?
- Do particular forms of celebrating and remembering influence or change the perception of today's Australia?

Further reading

If you would like to explore the concept of communicative memory further and discover the differences between 'collective memory' and 'cultural memory', see www.goethe.de/ges/pok/dos/dos/ern/kug/en2984071.htm.

4. Memory in the curriculum plays

Collective and individual memories are an important component in all of the verbatim plays on the HSC list. The following work is best done in groups.

The Laramie Project
This play chronicles life in the town of Laramie in the year after Matthew Shepard's murder. In 2008, a decade after piecing together the play about his murder, 'the creators of the *The Laramie Project* returned to Wyoming to investigate the long-term cultural impact of the murder and the collective memory of the community a decade after the event'.[81]

- Who owns the memories which are acted out in *The Laramie Project* and *Epilogue*?
- Should *The Laramie Project* only be performed in Wyoming, for only those people who had a personal connection with the events?
- How could it be performed in your school or your neighbourhood? Could it be adapted to fit in with your local community? If so, how? If not, why not?

Aftershocks
This play is set amongst the community of the Newcastle Workers Club. The 1989 earthquake destroyed the Club, which had been the centre of trade union activity in Newcastle.

- Can memory assist in the rebuilding of a community?
- Could the title of this play have any metaphorical connection to the notion of memory and remembering? How?
- Would this insight affect the decisions on how to perform the various remembered stories? If so, how?
- Which performance strategies could be used to stress the importance of memory in the individual stories?

Parramatta Girls
The 2008 NSW Premier's Literary Awards Shortlists referred to Alana Valentine's play as follows: 'When former inmates of the Girls Training School, Parramatta, attend a reunion inside the now-closed institution, a dark body of individual and collective memory surfaces.' According to the text, the play is set in 2003 and 'in the remembered past', which is partly shared via the stories told on stage.

- Explore ways of sharing 'the remembered past' with the audience in both verbal and non-verbal ways.
- When doing so, how do you prevent the 'scabs' of the original inmates from hurting again?

Run Rabbit Run
In the playscript's introduction, titled 'A Bridge from Sport to Art', Chris Mead writes that the play 'seeks to be a work of oral and performative history.

Mitchell Butel, Josef Ber, Alicia Talbot, Eliza Logan, Tara Morice, Lynette Curran and Russell Dykstra in the 2001 Company B production of *The Laramie Project*. (Photo: Heidrun Löhr)

It is about celebrating difficult events of the recent past in an attempt to understand the history of the present, beyond media bias or compression'.

- How can the past help in understanding the present?
- How can the importance of the past be shown on the stage?
- Which strategies are most suitable for showing a past 'beyond media bias'?

Minefields and Miniskirts
This play contains numerous memories of violence with both physical and psychological trauma, not surprising since these recollections are derived from a war zone. The play paints vivid images based on memories that would have been more than twenty years old at the time oral historian Siobhan McHugh conducted her interviews.

- What do you think happens to memories over time?
- Why might this be important to a verbatim playwright?
- Is a memory of violence special in some way?

5. *Memory, authenticity and truth*

In the introduction to *Aftershocks*, Paul Brown makes the following observation about the initial interviews in preparation for the verbatim play: 'It is important to note that Club staff had, by this stage, told and re-told their stories many times—to each other, to the press, to counsellors, and to an Inquiry'.

Exercises

- Return to the very first activity. Without using any notes or prompts, retell your memories of the past event which you had acted out before.
- Have you changed the way you told the story? Discuss this in your group. Focus on the words, tone of voice, gestures, and body language which you have used.
- In your opinion, was your first version of sharing your memories authentic and true? What about your second version – was this false and constructed? Why or why not?
- Do you think your answers also apply to the interviews conducted for *Aftershocks*?
- Do you see any connection between retelling memories and Chinese whispers?

Depending on your answers to the questions above, you might agree or disagree with the statement that there is no such thing as authentic memory, particular when it is communicated to others. This partly explains the phenomenon that sporting achievements and fish caught by fishermen tend to grow in importance and size when retold several times!

As Susanne Knaller has explained, authenticity is a concept that has been introduced in the sense of artistic or author authenticity only in the twentieth century. While the term has been defined in multiple ways, there seems to be some consistency regarding its association with something or someone 'truthful', 'essential', 'unmediated' and 'genuine'. In discussion of verbatim plays, 'authenticity' may also refer to the sense of being close to the real person whose story is being told. This may include the sense that an audience has 'immediate' access to a real person's language.[82]

6. An *'authenticity contract'* between performers and audiences

The effective staging of 'authentic' memories relies on collective processes of certifying authenticity. To give an example, audiences might perceive the colloquial language used by some footy team supporters as 'authentic', particularly if the notion of 'immediate' access to everyday, unpolished language is reinforced by pauses, repetitions, 'ums' and 'ahs'.

This 'authenticity contract' between performers and audiences needs to be repeated in each relevant instance. This means that your audiences implicitly agree that each performance of your group's memories, and each witness' individual story or story segment, will take place under the premise of authenticity.[83] As actors know, seeming as though you have 'learnt' your text and you're mechanically repeating it will dismantle the sense that you are relating 'authentic memories'.

Exercise

Following are two versions of a speech: one from *Aftershocks* and a variation. The first is from Scene 4: Stan's ride, in which Stan Gill is injured in the earthquake.

> **STAN:** I remember I looked at him, while it was going on, we could hear this massive roar, this sorta, huge, like a bloody underground train coming... and then we stopped talking... There was three big, long slow waves, and the whole floor just collapsed.

Have several members of the group perform this speech and discuss why it might be described as 'authentic' (or not). Next, have a look at the following text.

> **STAN:** I remember looking at him while the earthquake was going on. All along, we could hear a massive roar, which sounded as though an underground train were coming. It was at this point that we stopped talking. Subsequently there were three big, long slow waves. To my horror, the whole floor collapsed.

You may find it hard to put your finger on why the two versions produce different understandings of authenticity and 'truth'. Maybe it feels like the direct connection to a real person's view of the world is lost in the second, 'cleaned-up' version. Do you agree? Does it matter?

Further reading

Interestingly, in one of the plays set for the curriculum, *Minefields and Miniskirts*, we are able to explore the above effect by studying the differences between the original transcribed interviews made by Siobhan McHugh and the versions performed in Terence O'Connell's adaptation for the stage. You can find examples in Siobhan McHugh's 2006 article, '*Minefields and Miniskirts*: the perils and pleasures of adapting oral history for the stage' published in the *Oral History Association* journal. Access this at http://ro.uow.edu.au/creartspapers/26.

Exercise

We can explore how the process of adapting real-life speech may have a positive effect in terms of enhancing the drama. As an example, read and then explore the tensions in this fragment of interview with Siobhan McHugh, talking with Roslyn Oades about *Minefields and Miniskirts*:

> **SIOBHAN:** Had it been a travesty, which was my greatest fear, I could have disassociated myself from it. But I had to accept the play is a different entity. Yes it is based on this work [the oral history interviews]. I would say that the script is probably ninety percent transcript from the interviews. I went through... I did a bit of a study to see where anything was different, or where Terence changed or stopped it where the transcript went somewhere else. And he certainly added certain things.
>
> **ROSLYN:** There are quite poetic lines, like I've noted one here: 'We were like diamonds in the dirt', which Sandy says on page 23?
>
> **SIOBHAN:** That's built on... Ingrid says, 'We were like diamonds', so Ingrid is the entertainer with the combat jacket here and she says, 'We were like diamonds, I was adored, I was wanted, I was this, I was that'. She says it like that. So he took that phrase, 'We were like diamonds', and he transposes it 'in the dirt'... he added that phrase. So that's artistic license and I think it's very valid and very effective.

Eliza Logan has performed in several verbatim plays. Following is her view on authenticity in language.

> **ROSLYN:** How is working on a verbatim play different from working on a piece of imagined text?
>
> **ELIZA:** The main difference would definitely have to be that you get the rhythm of the language and the rhythm of the person – the specific person that's talking. So that you get their 'ums'

and 'ahs' their dot-dot-dots. I mean, whether the transcriber is actually incredibly accurate at doing that you don't know. You also don't necessarily get inflection. And with specifically the 'ums' and 'ahs' and very specific kind of local language, you get an insight into that specific person. With a written play or an imagined play, the writing can be, I guess, almost more 'classy'. It's more succinct, a lot of the time. I mean the writer can also potentially write something that seems incredibly real but I think, as humans, and generally everyday humans that aren't used to speaking on a public platform... that people that appear in these plays specifically, aren't necessarily concise. You know, it takes a lot to formulate thought and to understand what you believe in or what drives you or how to explain something. Sometimes if it's raw and quite emotional it takes quite a while to get it out. So I think there are examples in these plays where people kind of keep trying to get what they believe out, but they kind of go about it in three different ways until eventually, they go, 'Ah! Now I know what I'm talking about'. I think that's quite beautiful. You don't get that in a written play.

7. Performing memories: Which memories? Whose memories? For whom?

You might want to complete your activities in this section by considering the people involved in the performance of memories.

Exercise

- Which role would you like the audiences to play in your verbatim performances?
- Do you consider your audiences to be quiet witnesses?
- Do you want them to share the memories? How?
- Would you like them to develop a critical attitude towards an issue? If so, how do you invite them to develop a critical attitude towards selected segments of your performances?

When sharing memories on stage, you can provide local communities or even national cultures with a stronger and continuous sense of identity, community and belonging (See Chapter 14: Verbatim Theatre and Community). On the other hand, there are many other stories which do not get told; or there might even be a conscious effort to 'forget' other people's stories.

Exercise

- Whose memories and stories would you like to tell?

- Which of your own memories would you like your grandchildren to remember?
- Would you choose to tell these memories in a verbatim play? Why or why not?
- Discuss the limits and opportunities of choosing a verbatim play for sharing memories. How are these limits and opportunities apparent in the plays on the reading list?

13.

Theatricality and Engagement: Performing Real People

Workshop by Meg Mumford

This workshop poses a number of questions for exploration in small groups about how actors and other creative artists engage with verbatim plays. Discussion about this will evolve on the Currency website.

Questions to be addressed

The ideal approach is for participants to skim the questions then read the selection of extracts from interviews with the creative artists involved in the five set curriculum plays. Then return to each question in detail, through discussion and/or experimentation 'on your feet'.

What is the nature and implication of the performer's personal contact with the interviewee?

- Is it desirable that the actors meet the people whose stories they are telling?
- Should the actors be the interviewers, and what difference will it make if they are?
- In a verbatim play made from interview transcripts, should the cast and crew listen to audio and/or visual recordings of the interviews?
- What might it be like for the interviewees to visit the rehearsal room?
- What expectations arise when the 'real people' attend a performance?

How will the performer approach the task of presenting a real living subject?

- Will actors try to reproduce physical mannerisms or vocal characteristics?
- What about a more psychophysical imitation involving empathetic processes?
- How does performing verbatim compare with, for example, Brechtian or comic defamiliarisation, mixing empathy and estrangement, making a satirical caricature, or other approaches to making a character?

What is the importance of the performer's social relationship and attitude to the interviewee?

- Is the relationship between performers and the characters they play different for some reason in verbatim theatre?
- Would it make for a better performance if the actor had a similar social background to that of the person whose story is being told?
- To what extent is the performer responsible to the interviewee for 'telling the story the right way'?

Creative artists' comments on performing verbatim

Here are selected extracts from interviews with writers, directors and other creative artists who have worked on Australian verbatim plays. The full interviews, conducted by Roslyn Oades, are available on the Currency Press Verbatim website. Read these in detail, then return to the questions above.

> Yeah the best way to think about performing *Aftershocks* is to say to yourself as an actor, 'Well, I'm not trying to transform into this person, I'm trying to tell the story to the audience'. As soon as you identify as a storyteller rather than as an actor transforming, it feels a lot easier to just walk out to the audience and make an announcement, 'Howard and Elaine's story' and then you might step a little bit to one side and you signify to the audience that you've finished making an announcement and now we're going to do the story.
>
> **Paul Brown, playwright, Aftershocks**

> The actor [is] confronting the audience as the actor... I guess embracing what we would now consider to be a more Brechtian style of work, where the actor is always the actor and they report the words of the character. The transformation process is taken out, [but] that doesn't mean there isn't magic and entertainment and all of those things that we love about theatre... but that the actor themselves is very present in the theatre-making task each night. The character doesn't take over. And something like *The Laramie Project* has X amount of characters, only a handful of which are continual, so the actors are having to present the testimony of a number of different characters across the two or three hours of the project... There's always illusion... there's suspension of disbelief but it is instant. Someone puts on a pair of glasses and says, 'I'm Zackie Salmon' then we have to believe that. We simply believe her without judgment. The actor is presenting the spirit of that person without judgment.
>
> **Kate Gaul, director, 2001 Company B production of The Laramie Project**

Jacqui Phillips and John Jarratt in the 1993 Company B production of *Aftershocks*. (Photo: Paul Wright)

You find a lot of style, I guess, about delivery, from what they say and then, of course, their voices are a bit different and then their physicality gestures are going to be a bit different. Posturally, yes, I was a bit different with a couple of them. I know that Romaine was kind of quite upright and sporty – Sporty Spice – and kind of a bouncy physicality. Aaron was a teenage boy who was talking about something very difficult so, you know, from a bit hunchy and a bit sort of like 'I don't necessarily want to be having to tell you this information'... I played [the little girl] as well. She had quite sort of spiritual things to say and quite sort of deep. She was pretty full on, like a young girl who was really daring to say some pretty heavy stuff. And we used a scarf as well. So that kind of changes your physicality as well. She's a young uni student... I just had my normal clothes on underneath and then this scarf.

Eliza Logan, actor,
2001 Company B production of *The Laramie Project*,
2004 Company B production of *Run Rabbit Run*

I think the biggest challenge was keeping the actors confident about being able to speak to the audience. Working through a number of disparate characters. To trust the structure and to trust that the simplicity with which we were doing... with which we were manifesting these characters would work. I think that was the biggest creative challenge... although the characters or the voices of the play are based on living people, probably who are still alive, creating the play still enacted the imagination first and foremost. [For the actors in *The Laramie Project* at Belvoir] to go and meet the real people was not of any use imaginatively as far as I'm concerned. I had met the people from Laramie and I knew also whether the members of the Tectonic Theatre Project were male or female but I let the actors make up their own minds about those things, because I don't think... it didn't alter the fabric of the play. The more imaginative it was, the better.

Kate Gaul

Yeah, well the thing is, the premise that it's actually been created is an intimate one. So in the interview process, when the people have created the work, they are having a discussion over a table with a microphone or a tape recorder and it's quite personal. So when it comes to performing that, you could potentially recreate that world but why do that when you can use the audience as the interviewer? So in that respect, yes, it breaks that fourth wall instantly. That's if you choose to perform it that way. And I'd hope you did, 'cause it's a much more intimate experience for the audience as well... But then it's the story that takes focus and it sort of sits in this kind of bubble between you. Like the memory sits there. So you're basically reliving that memory and they are capturing it. Because it's you talking about something that's happened in the past and it unlocks a lot of emotional... you know, if you're sitting in the shoes of something who's had the experience like that, it's pretty full on. You kind of... it starts with just telling someone a story but the more intense it gets the more it becomes this kind of like the whole room becomes the interviewer.

Eliza Logan

The audience is obviously very clever and when they're sitting in a verbatim play they come away with some idea that this is real life. They know there was an earthquake in Newcastle... They know that they're expecting 'reality'. So that whole thing of suspending of disbelief which audiences are supposed to do when they enter the theatre is a bit different in verbatim. I think what you're doing is you're opening yourself up to receive two types of story or two versions of the same story. You're getting what the actor is telling you and you can enjoy that on the level of performance that's here for you now. But you're also continually aware that that's story arising from the words of a real person... Or you can feel it, you can feel that this is different sort of speech; it's vernacular or whatever. So you can open yourself to hearing both the voice of the real person and the voice of the actor.

Paul Brown

Most of it's direct address to the audience and you never get a chance to rehearse with an audience so it's extremely, extremely hard to rehearse these kinds of plays. I think the director's job in a sense is to look at the overall rhythm of it, to find out what the shape of it is and how that can actually fit with your team of actors. It's very hard for an actor to keep talking to the air. I mean, you can do it to each other – it's always about action and intention and objective and all of those things ring true. And then it's just the mechanics of how do we actually do it. But it's difficult to rehearse because there were no actual dramatic scenes. The audience is your scene partner and you never get to rehearse with those people.

Kate Gaul

The thing that I don't think an audience should ever forget is that they're in a theatre. I think it's wonderful if they're taken away somewhere else, but that's in their mind. You're not in someone's bedroom... I think what I found true of verbatim theatre is that you set up a comfortable place for the actors to be, so that when they are the characters, it's a comfortable situation: it's not damaged and it's not affected in any way that the characters might be or the situation was. *Laramie* was just a series of tables and chairs.

Brian Thomson, designer,
1993 Company B production of **Aftershocks**,
2001 Company B production of **The Laramie Project**,
2004 Company B production of **Run Rabbit Run**

The theatre event is in the present. Aha! This taps into a very interesting question: the event happened in the past but the theatre happens in the present and that's one of the challenges of *The Laramie Project*: what is happening now. All of the events have happened in the past of any of these plays and we all know the outcome. But the play happens in the present and we must never forget that. So what makes it hard for the actors is, 'So, what's happening now?' 'I'm telling you about something that, A, you already know about, B, you know the outcome was... so what am I doing now? What am I doing?' It's really, really hard. So, 'Why am I telling you this story? What do I want from you? And how am I going to get it?' is still a core part of the creative task, if you like. And it's really, really hard.

Kate Gaul

14.
Verbatim Theatre and Community
WORKSHOP BY JAMES ARVANITAKIS

Previous chapters have outlined some of the important aspects of verbatim theatre, including the importance of telling 'real life' and often 'untold' stories. There is another important dimension noted in Part One of this book that we will now turn to: the link between verbatim theatre and 'community'. That is, we will explore how verbatim theatre projects have the potential to create, reaffirm and challenge established concepts of and within communities.

What is community?

The place to start is to consider the concept of 'community'. The idea of community crosses all political divides, and we can observe that conservative, reactionary, progressive and radical groups all invoke the concept of community. For example, those who promote globalisation and the free market argue that these mechanisms result in the formation of a 'global community', with increased opportunities, shared understandings and, ultimately, peace.[84] Meanwhile those who oppose the 'free market' or are 'anti-globalist' also summon community but take the opposite position: that such processes threaten or diminish local communities. Having a community, or at least a 'community of interest', is widely regarded as valuable in solving social problems, which is why both government and non-government sectors also embrace community, seeking the 'magic' ingredient that will lead to 'community building'.

According to community worker Jeremy Brent, community is something that is always called upon when social problems are experienced;[85] and Zygmunt Bauman argues our craving for community is 'like a roof under which we shelter in heavy rain, like a fireplace [where] we warm our hands on a frosty day'.[86]

Despite such a longing for the stability and warmth of community, we need to see it as a double-edged sword; it can produce co-operation and mutuality, but can also be divisive and create conflict. For example, when bush fires ravaged Victoria in early 2009 resulting in dozens of deaths, the 'Australian community' pulled together to raise funds and assist the victims. In stark contrast, the concept of community was used as an excuse to attack 'outsiders' during the Cronulla race riots, in Sydney's southern beachside suburbs. In the first example, community crossed all divides; in the case of

Cronulla, a sense of community excluded those with the 'wrong' skin colour, religion or ethnicity.[87]

We should think of community like 'oxygen': while it is something that we do not see or touch, its sense of existence or failure to materialise has a real impact on our lives.

How do communities develop?

Before talking about the role that theatre can have in establishing community, it is important to note that there are two broad conceptions about community formation.

The first revolves around 'recognition' and the concept that there exist 'natural communities' based on the concept that we form communities with those we 'recognise' as being 'like us'.[88] For example, this might mean forming community only with people of the same religion or skin colour or same coloured eyes or who speak the same language. 'Natural communities' refers to the dominant conceptualisation of community, and it envisages community relying on shared and mutual beliefs, understandings and practices – all seen to create a stable sense of identity.[89]

For theorist Francis Fukuyama, twin pillars support community. The first is 'citizenship' of a democratic state. Here, anyone who is issued with citizenship is accepted. The second pillar is associated with 'rational' self-interest that drives the free market. We are all part of an economy and recognise each other as a community of consumers and producers. Together, these help us form a community.[90] At no time, however, does Fukuyama problematise community – he merely sees it as something that forms naturally and with ease.

The alternative perspective is that community only forms through a sense of both difference and desire: that is, you have to 'want' to form a community with someone and this may require hard work and understanding. Further, rather than seeking others 'like us', we want to be seen as individuals and appreciated as such. Here, community is something that is not neat and easily defined, but something complicated.[91]

This second position is opposite the concept of natural communities formed around people 'like us'. The argument is that we don't actually have a real community if it can only be maintained by excluding people, which can ultimately lead to violence and oppression. For example, if we form a community with only those who speak the same language, what happens if one of us marries someone from outside the language group? Do we arrest this person or throw them out?

If we are prepared to answer 'no' to that last question, we are willing to see community formed through a desire to accept and be accepted, despite difference. This type of community is based on a sense of reciprocity: 'I want you to be part of my community and you want me to be part of yours, and so we work at establishing and maintaining it'.

Theatre and community

What does all this have to do with verbatim theatre? How do we link these issues with the various plays we have been studying in this book? That is, are verbatim plays merely reflections of already established 'natural communities', or do such projects also meet the broad and ambitious goals of bringing together different people and establishing a desire amongst the participants to form a new, inclusive community?

To answer this, we should first begin noting that one of the essential elements of verbatim theatre is that it brings together personal stories and links them with universal themes. It allows audiences to see the consequences of certain events on real people's lives. For example, *Aftershocks* is not only a play about those affected by the Newcastle earthquake, but it also conveys universal ideas about leadership, loss, dislocation, grief and what can appear as government indifference.

Looking at *The Laramie Project*, its focus is the issue of homophobic violence. If we follow the concept that community is based on recognition between people who are alike, we might think that the only people with interest in the play would be members of the gay community. However, the project's history indicates that the audience was drawn from much wider circles, to include those interested in prejudice and opposing acts of violence. The performance breaks down the idea that we can only relate to people 'like us' and creates a sense of desire to form a peaceful community.

Likewise, *Run Rabbit Run* relates to a specific rugby league team and you might think only 'Rabbitoh' supporters would be drawn in as audience. The 2004 'sell-out' season tells us that the motivations of those attending the play went beyond being a supporter of a football Club. Rather, the broader themes of people working together to overcome adversity had wider appeal.

Parramatta Girls is not only a play about some of the 500,000 Australians who experienced care in an orphanage over the twentieth century, but about truth and reconciliation. The production worked to create a desire for community between the broader audience and anyone we see struggling with issues of justice, as well as feeding into broader discussions regarding Australia's national identity and history.

Class discussion

- Return to each of the plays in this book and consider what you would believe to be the 'natural community' that each production would appeal to.
- Now discuss the broad (universal) themes of each play and reflect on how consideration of these might generate desire for community.
- Is there a contrast between the 'natural community' of the play, and the community suggested by considering universal themes? Why?

Lisa Flanagan and Leah Purcell in the 2007 Company B production of *Parramatta Girls*. (Photo: Heidrun Löhr)

- In other workshops, we have discussed the different stages required for producing a verbatim theatre performance. Discuss how these different elements can contribute to establishing a desire for community.
- How do plays such as *The Laramie Project* and *Minefields and Miniskirts* bring together communities that may be seen as 'oppositional'?
- Think of some recent incidents in contemporary Australia that have created controversy. Which would have the potential to be an interesting verbatim theatre project? Discuss how you would build a desire for community around such a project.

Additional exercise

Playwright Alana Valentine (*Parramatta Girls, Run Rabbit Run*) spoke with Roslyn Oades about the importance of community in verbatim work. (The full interview is available on the Currency Press Verbatim website.) Explore Valentine's ideas as a way of deepening the discussion:

> **ROSLYN:** I remember hearing strongly that, for you, verbatim has been a real commitment to a community.
>
> **ALANA:** Bringing the community along... is a big part of it for me. And there's a lot of work in that that doesn't necessarily go along with just a kind of tunnel vision commitment to the best play on stage. But that's not to say they're mutually exclusive. My commitment is always to the best play on stage. And my commitment in any interview is to getting the best story and the best material out of a person. It's a balancing act—
>
> **ROSLYN:** It's a responsibility.
>
> **ALANA:** Yeah, there's a responsibility there and there's also this sweet triumph. I mean, when you sit in the audience and all those women [who were Parramatta Girls in real life] go on stage and there's a standing ovation for them... there's nothing like it and you know you've done your job... I think it's part of the reward of verbatim... And it's wonderful and it is transformative of the community. You know the South Sydney community isn't a community until you sort of almost reflect it back to them and say... by saying they're a community, they become a community. And yes they sort of are a community but they're really a disparate group of individuals who pulled together for one thing and then dissipated. Then when you put them back on stage [as in *Run Rabbit Run*] and see them reflect the journey of their triumph, suddenly they re-understand what they've done

and re-experience their connection to other people in that process. So, theatre gifts that to them. Gifts the community back to itself...

ROSLYN: What was the journey for the community participants [in *Parramatta Girls*]?

ALANA: They loved being believed. That was the most important thing. You know, on the opening night, [one of the women] came up to me and said, 'You've given me back the twelve-year-old girl that was taken from me'... In terms of the community, I mean, all the news cameras and stuff wanted to do interviews with these girls and it was just great. I loved them having their story be so respected and believed. And I mean, clearly, for me, you know, the National Apology [to the Forgotten Australians] that happened was just the most extraordinary day for me as a theatre-maker. I texted Wesley Enoch and I said 'I think we can be proud to be theatre-makers on this day'. You know, CLAN [Care Leavers of Australia Network] and all of those groups had been agitating for a national apology. I'm not claiming any part in that. I'm just saying there was a small part of what we did for however many people came to the Belvoir Street Theatre, who understood in some way what had happened to those women. And who knows how much they might have been the friends or the mothers of people in positions of influence: who could help the rollercoaster that was already in place by CLAN and all these other groups to get the National Apology. I feel really proud of those women for gifting their story to all those other women who weren't given a voice, you know?... And the theatre can't resign its mantle of connecting to what's happening in our community now.

15.
Ethics, Ownership, Authorship
WORKSHOP BY PAUL BROWN

Through three activities and associated commentary, this workshop aims to provide practical advice about how to deal with a range of ethical issues in verbatim theatre projects.

Let's say you make up a story and you write it down. I'm talking about something you invent yourself, a fabrication which involves fictional characters, with a plot that isn't someone's real life story. Who 'owns' that story? Well it's fairly certain you do! Our instincts about what is 'fair' suggest that it's your story, and lawfully, through provisions for 'copyright', it is also yours. You can legally claim the 'copyright' in the written work, meaning that it's yours to trade or exploit, perhaps to sell to a producer of films or plays, or to another writer who wants to adapt your work.

But what about the stories that make up verbatim plays? Who 'owns' them? Or 'Who is the author of the play?' These questions are complicated enough (see Activity 1 below), but it becomes potentially even more complex when the play is made in a community development context, and/or when groups of people share the same story, or when one community member retells the story of another.

Activity 1

Think about this: A real person, who has a story to tell, relates the story to a researcher or creative artist, often via an interview tape. The same creative artist, or maybe others, make a transcript, then edit this into a (written) playscript. This script is used to make a performance, which could be a play, and/or possibly a film or radio broadcast.

- Story, tape, transcript, playscript, performance... who do you think should own each of these elements in the creative process?
- And who would you describe as the 'author' of the finished play? Discuss this in small groups.

There is no single answer, but there are processes which can be used to find the right answer for each project. One approach is to first establish who will be responsible for managing issues of ownership, copyright and authorship. Maybe there is one 'independent' person designated to do this, or perhaps such management is a function of a 'steering group' if the project has one. The overall aim is to consult people involved, heading towards agreements about who owns what and who should be attributed as 'author'. This same group may also take on the job of considering other ethical questions likely to be associated with verbatim projects (see below).

The second, and very important, approach is to make a written agreement or contract with the people involved. Sometimes such a contract is called a 'release form', and it is common for verbatim playwrights to use one in order to establish what they can and can't do with the stories they are being told; also to record how people will be acknowledged and who will be regarded as the 'author'. Appendix 2 contains two sample release forms. By the way, documentary filmmakers also use release forms when they do interviews. Journalists sometimes do too, though it is rare. Keep in mind that separate agreements will be needed with other members of the creative team, since, under law, someone who conducts an interview and makes a transcript has copyright in that interview.

However, it would be a mistake to think it all boils down to ownership and contracts. Verbatim work raises a wider range of ethical issues. Let's keep in mind that most plays deal with sensitive and traumatic material. It's what makes them good drama, but the lives of real people, not fictional characters, are sometimes literally at stake. There are clear-cut cases. Sometimes certain story fragments cannot be used because to do so would endanger legal proceedings. (Journalists face this kind of thing all the time, and they are bound by codes of practice.) Then come the problems faced by both interviewee and interviewer in verbatim work, namely that the interview itself can be traumatic if it involves recounting sensitive events. That's why in some projects, great care is taken to 'debrief' after interviews.

Activity 2

This time think about what it would be like to tell a playwright one of your own personal stories, perhaps one that you've kept secret from most people.

- Would you feel uneasy about a stranger knowing?
- What if your story was then edited so that only certain parts were used? Would you want a say in how that was done?
- How would you feel if your story was assigned to a 'composite' character? (Most verbatim plays do this to some extent. See as examples *Parramatta Girls* and *Minefields and Miniskirts*.)
- Let's say you were quite pleased to have your story used and edited for a performance in your own community... would you feel differently if it became part of a play produced in other parts of Australia and seen by thousands of people, or a film seen by millions?
- Would you want your own name attached to the story, or would you want to remain anonymous?
- If you mention other people in your story, do you think you would need their permission?

One contentious issue is the extent to which the people whose story is being told should be involved in the editing process and other elements of play-making. Again, the answer lies in establishing agreed and tailor-made processes, rather than in any one solution. Release forms may stipulate that original storytellers are able to comment on script drafts, or to receive the transcript of their interview for checking, to allow them right of veto over particular material they don't want used. It is very common in verbatim play development to 'play back' the draft script to the people whose stories are being told, through preliminary readings and 'closed' performances. These are great opportunities to put everyone at ease with how the material is being used. In my experience, most people very generously prefer to see a great story dramatised as a piece of structured 'collective memory' (see Chapter 12: Memory, Truth and Authenticity), in which their own story is a part of a whole and therefore edited and shaped within that whole. They are less concerned about having every detail of their own experience preserved.

Activity 3

The experience of making *Aftershocks* provides another model for you to critique. The play dramatises the collapse of the Newcastle Workers Club during the 1989 earthquake and is made from interviews with staff and patrons of the Club. The Newcastle Workers Cultural Action Committee, based at the Club, initiated the project.

- In considering ethical issues, a steering committee of trade unionists and Club workers consulted then agreed that ownership of the stories should be shared amongst the original storytellers and the creative artists.
- This led to a written agreement that any earnings from the play, should be split 50:50 between the playwright and the Workers Cultural Action Committee representing the original storytellers.
- The release form covered how interviews could be used, and it dealt with ownership of story. It also stipulated that if and when the play became a film, which it did in 1998, a further negotiation would be needed, and this led to new contracts with the original storytellers.
- On the question of authorship, the agreement was that the playwright and the Workers Cultural Action Committee would be stated as the authors in all publicity and on the playscript.
- Part of the *Aftershocks* process was a preliminary reading of the draft play to an audience of people whose stories were being told. Feedback from that group influenced the selection of stories and reinforced the overall direction the play was beginning to take.
- Various negotiations took place between the creative team and the original storytellers. For example one person wanted to remain

anonymous in the playscript. Another person asked for anonymity when the play became a film.

Discuss the benefits and the pitfalls in the above approach to matters of ownership of story.

Appendix 1: Interview Technique

Verbatim theatre practitioners learn a great deal from oral historians about interview techniques. Here, Roslyn Oades asks Siobhan McHugh, oral historian on *Minefields and Miniskirts*, about her techniques.[92]

ROSLYN: What makes for good interview material?

SIOBHAN: I think just naked truth and somebody who can actually recreate the sense of what it was like to be someone. They can put themselves back in their young person's point of view. And I actually try and do that as an interviewer. I employ gut-psychology and stuff like that when framing the questions in order to try and bring somebody into that frame of mind. To change them from the complacent fifty-year-old, suburban mother, perhaps, that's sitting in front of me and to bring her back to that knife edge person of twenty-three she once was. I plan my questions in such a way that it actually makes them go back on a journey. I also try and create that real sense of heightened intimacy that you can get. I've written a paper about it: 'The Aerobic Art of Interviewing'.[93] That describes all of my techniques as an interviewer.

ROSLYN: I was going to ask what your advice for conducting an interview is?

SIOBHAN: Obviously the first thing is research. It is much better to not just be fishing vaguely for information. If I was going to interview a nurse, I'd try and find out what was the set-up medically, what did they have, how advanced were x-rays or did they have intensive care units at that time. I'd try to do a bit of background reading and stuff like that. But of course the interview process is also a form of research. Interview number one will feed into research for interview number five so actually the interview that you do with number twenty-five is far more honed in a way and you're asking them things that you got from previous interviews. So it does feed off itself.

ROSLYN: And then you mentioned intimacy being important. I imagine that the base of intimacy is knowledge.

SIOBHAN: That's right. I think the keys to a good interview are research, curiosity, empathy and, what I call 'aerobic listening', [which] perfectly describes what we do. When somebody's talking to me during an oral history interview, I feel like my ears are out on stalks because I'm actually hearing

Debra Byrne, Tracy Mann, Wendy Stapleton, Tracy Bartram and Robyn Arthur in the 2004 Playbox Theatre production of *Minefields and Miniskirts*. (Photo: Lisa Tomasetti)

what they're saying and listening and being empathetic and, at the same time, I'm trying to see where does it connect to any questions that are either there or not that I need to ask. I'm also processing it for any seeming anomalies, either that I just need to clarify or where, in certain situations I might be fed misinformation. It's like you clone yourself down the middle and one of you is sitting there, [nodding] and listening and being interested and curious and that's enough for most people because just having an engaged audience is a great privilege for most of us. I mean, right now, I'm enjoying it. [Laughter]

ROSLYN: Oh, good.

SIOBHAN: But then the other part is almost simultaneously, already, working on processing that stuff and feeding it back in to the research questioning process. That combination of intense listening and focus creates this intimacy that's so different. An interview is not the same as a conversation. It's always different when you turn the tape recorder off... [You hear] this whole, 'Ahhh' sort of sigh.

ROSLYN: You hope they don't tell you their best story then.

SIOBHAN: Yeah!

Alex Sideratos, Russell Kiefel and Wayne Blair in the 2004 Company B production of *Run Rabbit Run*. (Photo: Heidrun Löhr)

Appendix 2: Sample Interview Release forms

urban theatre projects

Urban Theatre Projects Ltd
ABN 42 002 865 787
P.O. Box 707 Bankstown NSW 1885,
Tel: 02 9707 2111 Fax: 02 9707 2166
Email: mail@urbantheatre.com.au
Web: urbantheatre.com.au

INTERVIEWEE RELEASE FORM

Name of Interviewee: ....
Address: ....
....
Post code: ....
Phone: ....
Email: ....
Date of Interview: ___ / ___ / ___

I, the Interviewee, agree to grant Urban Theatre Projects
An interview (the Interview); and
The right to make an audio and/or visual recording of my interview (the Recording).
I assign all rights in the reproduction of my interview for the sole purpose of a verbatim-style theatre production to be directed by Roslyn Oades. I understand that this material may also be reproduced in video, audio or literary form for promotional and documentary reasons associated with this theatre project.
As acknowledgment of my contribution, I would like my real name credited in a show program produced for a public season of the theatre production:

YES / NO

I would like to be kept informed of performance dates for the project:

YES / NO

Accepted and agreed:
Signature of the interviewee: ....
If you require any further information regarding this project, please contact Urban Theatre Projects on 02 9707 2111

Newcastle Workers Cultural Action Committee
AFTERSHOCKS
LETTER OF AGREEMENT ABOUT A TAPED INTERVIEW

Name: ....
Address: ....
Phone: ....

The Workers Cultural Action Committee (WCAC) is a sub committee of Newcastle Trades Hall Council. It aims to provide cultural activities for workers and their families.

In 1991 WCAC will present a performance about the Newcastle Earthquake, that will draw on the experiences of people associated with the Workers Club, and others who have stories to tell about the earthquake and its aftermath.

As part of the research for the project, WCAC is interviewing a number of people on tape, and we thank you for contributing your taped interview. WCAC needs your permission to transcribe the interview, and make appropriate use of it in the following ways:

1. As background research material for a play.
2. As speeches to be included verbatim in a script for a play, and spoken by actors during a stage performance. Note: the speeches will need to be edited for this purpose.
3. As part of an archive of material to be kept by WCAC, for the use of genuine researchers and historians.
4. As part of an archive to be kept by public libraries and other organizations with oral history collections throughout Australia.
5. For broadcast on radio within a program about the earthquake.
6. For publication in a book.

Please delete any of the above uses that you do not want to authorize.

I agree to my interview being used in the above ways.

I also agree that copyright in the material will be owned jointly by myself and the interviewer, and that such copyright is licensed to WCAC and the Writer for the project, Paul Brown, for the uses listed above.

I do/do not give my permission for my name to be attributed to extracts from the transcripts or recordings involving myself and the interviewer.

I will receive a copy of the transcript of the interview.

I will be consulted by WCAC about any use of the material other than listed above.

Signed ....
    (Interviewee) on .... (date)
Countersigned ....
    (Interviewer) on..................................... (date)

Endnotes

1. Robin Soans in *Verbatim Verbatim: Contemporary Documentary Theatre* Eds. Will Hammond and Dan Steward. London: Oberon Books 2008, p.32.
2. Derek Paget, '"Verbatim Theatre": Oral History and Documentary Techniques' *New Theatre Quarterly* 3.12 (1987): 317–336, p.317.
3. Paget, p.317, original emphasis.
4. Hammond and Steward, p.9.
5. Dan Issac, 'Theatre of Fact' *The Drama Review* 15.3a (1971): 109–135.
6. Emily Mann, 'In Conversation' *Theatre Topics* 10.1 (2000): 1–16.
7. Dave Rogers, 'Banner Theatre: What Kind of Theatre?' www.bannertheatre.co.uk/what_kind_of_theatre.htm
8. Peter Weiss, 'The Material and the Models: Notes Towards a Definition of Documentary Theatre.; trans. Heinz Bernard *Theatre Quarterly* 1. 1 (1971): 41–43.
9. Attilio Favorini, 'Introduction: After the Fact: Theater and the Documentary Impulse' *Voicings: Ten Plays from the Documentary Theater* Ed. Attilio Favorini. New Jersey: Ecco Press 1995, p.xx.
10. Favorini, p.xxxi.
11. Janelle Reinelt, 'The Promise of Documentary' *Get Real: Documentary Theatre Past and Present* Ed. Alison Forsyth and Chris Megson. Basingstoke: Palgrave Macmillan 2009, p.13.
12. Reinelt, p.14.
13. Carol Martin, 'Bodies of Evidence' *TDR: The Drama Review* 50.3 (2006): 8–15, p.12.
14. Reddick in Georg Büchner, *Complete Plays, Lenz and Other Writings* trans. and notes by John Reddick. London: Penguin 1993, p.211.
15. D.G. Richards, *Georg Büchner and the Birth of Modern Drama*. Albany: State University of New York 1997, p.117.
16. Favorini, p.xviii.
17. Favorini, p.xvii-xix.
18. Derek Paget, 'Documentary Drama and Theatre' *The Oxford Encyclopedia of Theatre and Performance* Ed. Dennis Kennedy. Vol 1. Oxford: Oxford University Press 1993, pp.379–380.
19. Brian Barton, *Das Dokumentartheater* Stuttgart: Metzler 1987. Ulrike Garde's translation.
20. Ulrike Garde, p.266.
21. Favorini, p xxxiv.
22. Favorini, p.xxxviii. (He indicates that this would be a matrilineal approach, rather than an 'official' patrilineal theatre history.)
23. Della Pollock (ed.), *Remembering: Oral History Performance*. Basingstoke: Palgrave Macmillan 2005.
24. There is a vast literature on performance ethnography. For a good introduction see Norman K. Denzin's *Performance Ethnography: Critical Pedagogy and the Politics of Culture Thousand Oaks*: Sage Publications 2003.
25. Richard Norton-Taylor's 2007 play, one of a group of verbatim plays produced in the wake of Britain's involvement in the invasion of Iraq.

26. Robin Soans explores this in *Verbatim Verbatim: Contemporary Documentary Theatre* Eds. Will Hammond and Dan Steward. London: Oberon Books, 2008.
27. Stafford-Clark in Hammond and Steward.
28. Soans in Hammond and Steward, p.41.
29. David Hare responding to the Tribunal play *The Colour of Justice*, in Hare's important book Obedience, Struggle and Revolt, London: Faber and Faber, 2005
30. Nicholas Kent in Hammond and Steward, p.152.
31. Richard Norton-Taylor in Hammond and Steward, p.129.
32. Richard Norton-Taylor in Hammond and Steward, pp.123–4.
33. Lisa Bornstein, 'Turbulent Epic Tantalus Rose Above Crop of Good Productions', *Rocky Mountain News* 24 December 2000, p.15D.
34. Alisa Solomon, 'The Making of Americans', *Village Voice* 12 December 2000, p.152.
35. 'The Best and Worst of 2000: Theater', *Time Magazine* 18 December 2000, p.86.
36. Bryce Hallett, 'The Stuff of Shakespeare, In Ragged, Windy Wyoming', *Sydney Morning Herald* 16 March 2001, p.16.
37. Colin Rose, 'Brutal But Brilliant', *Sun Herald* 18 March 2001, p.13
38. John McCallum, 'Scene of the Crime Revisited', *Australian* 16 March 2001, p.11.
39. Phillip McCarthy, 'Consciences Get Rattled When Homophobia Rides Into Town', *Sydney Morning Herald* 15 March 2001, p.13.
40. Rose, p.13.
41. Michael Bodey, 'Diminishing the Dramatic Message', *Daily Telegraph* 23 March 2001, p.116.
42. Bodey, 'Diminishing', p.116.
43. Carrie Kablean 'Portrait of a Town', *Sunday Telegraph* 25 March 2001, p.109.
44. Nick Enright, '2002 Rex Cramphorn Lecture', 24 November 2002, p.4. www.currencyhouse.org.au/documents/ch_d_rex2002.pdf
45. Enright, p.4.
46. McCarthy, p.13.
47. Chelsea Clark, 'Entertainment News', *Daily Telegraph* 16 March 2001, p.107.
48. Peter Holder and Jo Casamento, 'Sydney Confidential', *Daily Telegraph* 26 March 2001, p.18.
49. Clark, p.107.
50. Hap Erstein, 'Hatred, American Style', *Palm Beach Post* 31 December 2000, p.1J.
51. *The Laramie Project* Epilogue is described at www.laramieproject.org
52. John McCallum, 'Scene of the Crime Revisited', *Australian* 16 March 2001, p.11.
53. Newcastle Regional Library, Local Studies and Information and Research Centre, 'Brief Facts and Figures', www.ncc.nsw.gov.au/discover_newcastle/local_history/newcastle_earthquake (5 June 2006).
54. Pamela Payne. 'Fault Lines', *Sydney Morning Herald* 12 July 1993, p.22. Brown had worked on large scale community theatre works, e.g. an ecological play with the Murray River Performing Group.
55. Paul Brown. '*Aftershocks*: Local Stories, National Culture' *Meanjin* 54.3 (1995): 449–60, p.458.
56. Paul Brown, '*Aftershocks*: Local Stories, National Culture' p.452; Brown, interview with Roslyn Oades.
57. Paul Makeham, 'Community Stories: *Aftershocks* and Verbatim Theatre' *Our Australian Theatre in the 1990s* Ed. Veronica Kelly. Amsterdam and Atlanta: Rodopi 1998, pp.168–81 p.171.

58. Paul Brown and the Workers Cultural Action Committee, *Aftershocks* (Second Edition). Sydney: Currency Press 2001 ppxx.
59. A full description of these areas and themes can be found in the Introduction.
60. Paul Brown, '*Aftershocks*: Verbatim Theatre About the 1989 Newcastle Earthquake: A Work in Progress' *Oral History Association of Australia Journal* 13 (1991): 49–55. p.51.
61. Paul Brown and Workers Cultural Action Committee, *Aftershocks* (Second Edition). Sydney: Currency 2001 p.35.
62. Paul Brown and Workers Cultural Action Committee, *Aftershocks* (First Edition). Sydney: Currency 1993 p.5.
63. Paul Brown, interview with Roslyn Oades. December 2009.
64. Angela Bennie, 'Courage Triumphs Amid the Chaos', *Sydney Morning Herald* 15 July 1993 p.17.
65. Paul Brown, 'NIDA Open Program: Verbatim Theatre Workshop', 2009.
66. Further information about Australian productions of the play can be found via the AusStage database website: www.ausstage.edu.au/advancedsearchresult.jsp?xcid=135 (2 April 2010).
67. Guy Rundle, 'Tragedy Told Simply' The *Age* 28 July 1995 p.19.
68. Angela Bennie, 'Courage Triumphs Amid the Chaos' *Sydney Morning Herald* 15 July 1993 p.17.
69. Elisabeth Wynhausen, 'Newcastle Quake Hits the Stage' *Sun Herald* 25 July 1993 p.38.
70. Paul Makeham, 'Community Stories: *Aftershocks* and Verbatim Theatre' *Our Australian Theatre in the 1990s* Ed. Veronica Kelly. Amsterdam and Atlanta: Rodopi 1998, pp.178–9.
71. John Murphy, 'Vietnam War', *The Oxford Companion to Australian History*, Eds. Davison, G. et al Revised Edition, Oxford: Oxford University Press 2001, pp.669–70.
72. Murphy, p.669.
73. The book had also been the basis of a radio series in 1993.
74. Siobhan McHugh, '*Minefields and Miniskirts*: the perils and pleasures of adapting oral history for the stage', *Oral History Association of Australia Journal*, 28, (2006) 22–29; access also at Research Online: http://ro.uow.edu.au/creartspapers/26
75. Interviews made by Roslyn Oades December 2009
76. Alana Valentine interviewed by Roslyn Oades in December 2009. This and all other quotes from Alana are extracts from that interview, which can be found on the Currency Press Verbatim website.
77. Chris Mead, 'A bridge from sport to art', *Run Rabbit Run* playscript by Alana Valentine. Sydney: Currency Press 2004, pp.x–xvii.
78. Wollongong Workshop Theatre staged an amateur production of *Run Rabbit Run* in 2006.
79. Nicholas Kent in *Verbatim Verbatim: Contemporary Documentary Theatre*. Eds. Will Hammond and Dan Steward. London: Oberon Books 2008, p.152.
80. Jan Assmann and John Czaplicka, 'Collective Memory and Cultural Identity', *New German Critique Cultural History/Cultural Studies* Spring– Summer (1995). pp.125–33.
81. An epilogue to *The Laramie Project* was created and performed worldwide in 2008. See http://arts.muohio.edu/theatre/call-board/news-archives/laramie-project.

82. Susanne Knaller, "authentisch/Authentizität", 45, in *Historisches Wörterbuch der ästhetischen Grundbegriffe*, Eds. Karheinz Barck, Martin Fontius et al. Stuttgart: Metzler 2005, pp.40–65.
83. Knaller, 47. See also Ulrike Garde, 'Spotlight on the audience: Collective creativity in recent Documentary and Reality Theatre from Australia and Germany' in Gerhard Fischer and Florian Vaßen (eds.), *Collective Creativity: Collaborative Work in the Sciences, Literature and the Arts*. Amsterdam, New York: Rodopi (forthcoming).
84. Thomas Friedman, *The world is flat*. New York: Farrar, Straus & Giroux 2005
85. Jeremy Brent, J. 'The desire for community: illusion, confusion and paradox', *Community Development Journal*, 39.3 (2004) pp.213–23.
86. Zygmunt Bauman, *Community: Seeking Safety in an Insecure World*. Cambridge: Polity Press 2001.
87. Scott Poynting, 'What caused the Cronulla Riot?', *Race and Class*, 48.1 (2006) pp.85–92.
88. Kelly Oliver, *Witnessing – beyond recognition*. Minneapolis: University of Minnesota Press 2001.
89. Charles Taylor, 'The politics of recognition', in Gutmann, Amy. (ed.) *Multiculturalism: examining the politics of recognition*, Princeton: Princeton University Press 1994.
90. Francis Fukuyama, F. 'Has History Started Again?', *Policy*, Winter 2002, pp.3–7.
91. Roslyn Diprose, 'Communities written in blood', *Cultural Studies Review*, 9.1 (2003), pp.35–50.
92. Siobhan McHugh interviewed by Roslyn Oades in December 2009
93. This paper can be accessed at http://ro.uow.edu.au/apme/vol1/iss18/13/

Bibliography

Individual chapters dealing with the set curriculum plays contain lists of resources for further study. What follows here is a more general listing of recommended background reading relevant to verbatim and documentary theatre.

Anderson, Michael and Linden Wilkinson. 'A Resurgence of Verbatim Theatre: Authenticity, Empathy and Transformation' *Australasian Drama Studies* 50 (2007): 153–169.

Barton, Brian. *Das Dokumentartheater*. Stuttgart: Metzler 1987.

Büchner, Georg. *Complete Plays, Lenz and Other Writings*, trans. and notes by John Reddick. London: Penguin 1993.

Denzin, Norman K. *Performance Ethnography: Critical Pedagogy and the Politics of Culture*. Thousand Oaks: Sage Publications 2003.

Favorini, Attilio. 'Introduction: After the Fact: Theater and the Documentary Impulse', *Voicings: Ten Plays from the Documentary Theater* Ed. Attilio Favorini. New Jersey: Ecco Press 1995.

Garde, Ulrike. *Brecht & Co. German-speaking Playwrights on the Australian Stage*. Bern, New York: Peter Lang 2007.

Hammond, Will, and Dan Steward (eds.), *Verbatim Verbatim: Contemporary Documentary Theatre*. London: Oberon Books 2008.

Innes, C.D. *Erwin Piscator's Political Theatre: The Development of Modern German Drama*. Cambridge: Cambridge University Press, 1972.

Isaac, Dan. 'Theatre of Fact', *The Drama Review* 15.3a (1971): 109–35.

Littlewood, Joan. *Joan's Book: Joan Littlewood's Peculiar History as She Tells It*. London: Methuen, 1994.

Mann, Emily. 'In Conversation', *Theatre Topics* Vol 10 No 1(2000): 1–16.

Martin, Carol. 'Bodies of Evidence' TDR: *The Drama Review*

McHugh, Siobhan. '*Minefields and Miniskirts*: the perils and pleasures of adapting oral history for the stage', *Oral History Association of Australia Journal*, 28, (2006) 22–29; access also at Research Online: http://ro.uow.edu.au/creartspapers/26

McInnes, Edward. *Lenz: Der Hofmeister*, Critical Guides to German Texts. London: Grant and Cutler, 1992.

McInnes, Edward. *'Ein ungeheueres Theater' The Drama of the Sturm und Drang*, Studien zur Deutschen Literatur des 19. und 20. Jahrhunderts, vol. 3. Frankfurt am Main: Peter Lang, 1987.

New South Wales Department of Education and Training, *HSC Drama Prescriptions* 2010–2012, www.curriculumsupport.education.nsw.gov.au/secondary/creativearts/assets/drama/pdf/verbatim.pdf

Osborne, John. *The Naturalist Drama in Germany*. Manchester: Manchester University Press, 1971.
Paget, Derek. 'Documentary Drama and Theatre' *The Oxford Encyclopedia of Theatre and Performance* Ed. Dennis Kennedy Vol 1 Oxford: Oxford University Press 2003, pp.379–80.
Paget, Derek. '"Verbatim Theatre": Oral History and Documentary Techniques' *New Theatre Quarterly* 3.12 (1987): 317–336.
Patterson, Michael. *The Revolution in German Theatre 1900–1933*. Boston: Routledge and Kegan Paul 1981.
Piscator, Erwin. *The Political Theatre*, trans. Hugh Rorrison. London: Eyre Methuen 1980.
Pollock, Della (ed.). *Remembering: Oral History Performance*. Basingstoke: Palgrave Macmillan 2005.
Reinelt, Janelle. 'The Promise of Documentary', *Get Real: Documentary Theatre Past and Present* .Eds. Alison Forsyth and Chris Megson. Basingstoke: Palgrave Macmillan 2009.
Rebellato, Dan. 'Naturalism', in Dennis Kennedy (ed.), *The Oxford Encyclopedia of Theatre and Performance*, vol. 2. Oxford: Oxford University Press 2003, pp.925–7.
Richards, D.G. *Georg Büchner and the Birth of the Modern Drama*. Albany: State University of New York, 1977.
Rogers, Dave. 'Banner Theatre: What Kind of Theatre?' Banner Theatre www.bannertheatre.co.uk/what_kind_of_theatre.htm
Samuel, Raphael, Ewan MacColl and Stuart Cosgrove. *Theatres of the Left 1880–1935: Workers Theatre Movements in Britain and America*. Boston: Routledge and Kegan Paul 1985.
Schumacher, Claude, ed. *Theatre in Europe: a Documentary History*, Cambridge: Cambridge University Press, 1996.
Weiss, Peter. 'Fourteen Propositions with Respect to the Documentary Theatre', *World Theatre/Theatre Dans le Monde* 17.5–6 (1968): 375–89.
Weiss, Peter. 'The Material and the Models: Notes Towards a Definition of Documentary Theatre'. Trans. Heinz Bernard *Theatre Quarterly* 1.1 (Jan-March 1971): 41–3.
Willett, John. *The Theatre of Erwin Piscator: Half a Century of Politics in the Theatre*. London: Methuen, 1986.

www.currency.com.au

Visit the Currency Press website now to:

- Buy your books online
- Browse through our full list of titles, from plays to screenplays, books on theatre, film and music, and more
- Choose a play for your school or amateur performance group by cast size and gender
- Obtain information about performance rights
- Find out about theatre productions and other performing arts news across Australia
- For students, read our study guides
- For teachers, access syllabus and other relevant information
- Sign up for our email newsletter

The performing arts publisher